". . . an inspiring example of the new generation of self-help books . . . the principles are universal in application . . . growth takes guts and that, as much as the sterling advice, is what this book is about."

David Alan Ramsdale,
MEDITATION Magazine

". . . moves the reader beyond the mechanics of recovery and into the living process of spiritual transformation . . . a deeply personal account of one woman's search for spiritual fulfillment through the dark passage of despair . . . . Its message is authentic."

Carol Riddle,
New Age WOMAN

The HEALING POWER of INNER LIGHT-FIRE

JANE EVANS LATIMER

Accessing Higher Consciousness to Transform Your Life

LivingQuest
Boulder, Colorado

For a free catalog or ordering information, contact:
LivingQuest
Box 3306
Boulder CO 80307
(303) 444-1319.

© 1990 by Jane Evans Latimer

Cover Design and Illustration by Ginny Pruitt, Benecia CA
Cover Photograph by Gene Latimer

Library of Congress Cataloging in Publication Data is available: LC Card Number 90-5492

Excerpt from Piero Ferrucci's book, *What We May Be*, by permission of Jeremy P. Tarcher, Inc., Los Angeles, © 1982 Piero Ferrucci.

Printed in the United States of America
10 9 8 7 6 5 4 3 2 1

Dedicated to the miracle of light within us all.

ACKNOWLEDGMENTS

This book was written with the assistance of many teachers, clients, friends and supporters. The following people spent their time reading early versions of the manuscript and giving invaluable feedback: Barbara Balock, Sharon Campbell, Violet Cleveland, Barbara Cohn, John Early, Barry Flint, Laurie Frain, Ben Fuchs, Paula Gannon, Martha Gooding, Jan Hestand, Willis Harman, Pam Hutchinson, Julie Jensen, Mary Jane Kelly, Mary Beth Kiefer, Stanley Krippner, Gay Luce, Chrystal Snyder Otto, George Pierson, John Poff, Sue Prentice, Penny Snyder, Alice Stearns and Anne Wilcox.

Thanks to Jan Kristiansson and John Kadlecek, who did an excellent job of organizing and editing; to Ginny Pruitt for her visionary cover illustration and design; and to Bob and Lee Evans, Meme Latimer, Penny Snyder and Marcus and Harryette Cohn for their generous support. To Gene, my husband, I send love and gratitude for eleven years of caring and encouragement, for our mutual child-rearing commitment and for a multitude of contributions to this book.

I am grateful for Russell and Carol Ann Schofield's vision, courage and ambition in forming the school of Actualism and to my teachers on the Actualism staff who stood steady in the light while I slowly and painstakingly learned the lessons necessary to heal — Elizabeth Barber, Wyndee Egan, Ginny Flint, Jan Hestand, Bruce Jaffe, Rebekah Lowden, Gil Messenger, Ralph Metzner, Lois Myerson, Penny Snyder, Dorothy Stephenson, Jon Terrell, Toby Weiss and especially Chrystal Snyder Otto who, in addition, encouraged me to find my own path of service. To my clients and workshop participants, I am grateful for the opportunity to be of service and to give back what I have received.

CONTENTS

FOREWORD

The process of psychological growth is an extraordinarily demanding creative enterprise, much like founding a business or producing a lifework of scholarship or designing artistic masterpieces. It is, in fact, the same type of effort. The masterwork of psychological transformation is the dramatic unfolding of both the apparent and hidden potentials of the personality.

The first step in this journey of change is to *become aware*. Indeed, this is a central component of psychotherapy: becoming aware of the layers of emotion, conflicting thoughts and perceptions that lie beneath our conscious awareness and motivate behavior. Making these heretofore invisible aspects of self visible, revealing the defense mechanisms and other psychic constructs that have kept them hidden, can bring a profound release. As the unrecognized is faced and acknowledged, an integration with once splintered parts of self is possible, invigorating the personality and opening new avenues of self-expression.

The resulting improvement, often momentous, can make it appear that simply becoming aware, "making the unconscious conscious," is all that is required to continue the process of transformation indefinitely. This is not the case. The next step is to experience the powerful energy of the higher self. In a healthy psyche, this force acts through the structures of the mind to energize the personality. However, trauma creates internal obstructions that cut off the flow of this vital power. The identity which has been thus robbed of life-energy can only be healed by a reconnection with the inner source: a rebirth into the presence of the divine that is deep within.

Many traditions of psychological and spiritual transformation make reference to the experience of light as crucial to moments of awakening or breakthrough. Light as illumination of the darkness, light as enlightenment of consciousness, light as a fire that cleanses the psyche. The reference to light is generally taken as symbol, a poetic way to describe a moment of epiphany. But there are those who look at the presence of light in these experiences literally rather than metaphorically: light-energy as the essential force of life. In this view, the light of the inner or higher self is the life energy that vivifies the substance of mind.

I first met Jane shortly after I moved to Manhattan in 1975. I was a young teacher of Actualism lightwork meditation training. She was an intense and passionate woman, looking for keys to her journey of self-directed growth.

Jane seemed to me a lot like New York itself, full of creative energy, volatile, almost constantly in a state of turmoil. Much of what we talked about in those early days was the conflicts she faced: wrestling with her past, struggling to survive in her job, in her relationships, in the city alone. And, above all, fighting with herself.

She saw the world as adversarial. Her conversation was laced with bitterness; shades of disappointment, panic and pain were the primary tonal qualities. She reached demandingly for hope, yet greeted each new suggestion with mistrust. *How do I know this will work? What if extending my awareness deeper within brings me more pain? I'm afraid I can't win against the negativity I feel inside me.*

Over the years, as our relationship has changed from teacher and student to friends and companions in the continuing exploration of the effects of inner light in our lives, I have had the privilege of witnessing Jane's transformation. She emerged from the torment of a long-standing eating disorder into a balanced, healthy lifestyle. The love she discovered within herself in this healing process led her to a marriage that is a strong partnership committed to spiritual growth. She has become a teacher and a counselor, using the insights from her own experiences to help others on their journeys of awakening.

This is what Jane's book is about: bringing the extraordinary power of inner centeredness into the ordinary flow of real life. It is about awakening to the transforming power of inner light. This light is the life within each of us, the glowing presence of the divine. From this source springs an unquenchable flow of life-renewing energy and life-affirming perspective.

If you have already found your path of inner growth, may this book touch you, as it did me, with the joy of recognition and the delight of shared understanding. If the perspectives presented here are new to you, may the reading open new windows for your mind and spirit.

Chrystal Snyder Otto
Scottsdale, Arizona
December 1989

AWAKENING
TO LIGHT

The story of my transformation began more than fifteen years ago when I sought a spiritual path that would help me break free of the dysfunctional behavior patterns that entrapped me. I remember standing outside the door of a mid-Manhattan apartment, about to embark on an experience which, little did I realize, was going to alter the rest of my life. I was welcomed by a middle-aged woman who showed me to my seat. Up front was a seemingly austere and quiet looking man. He seemed mysteriously detached, as if part of him were intently listening to and watching an inner world that I could neither see nor hear. He was tall, slim and erect; his movements, soft and careful. He seemed highly alert and sensitive — so unlike anyone I had known. I imagined him living in a different age — timeless, eternal and slow — when each moment glistened with the infinite stillness of rock and mountains.

My eyes wandered about the room. The walls were covered with books. The titles fascinated me: *In Search of the Miraculous, Telepathy, The Tibetan Book of the Dead, The Secret Science Behind Miracles.* These books were of another time and place, of another world, a world I wanted so much to enter but did not know how.

"Let us begin." His soft, deep voice startled me, taking me out of my reverie, drawing my attention to him again. This mysterious man seemed, in fact, to be of and live in the world I saw described in the book titles on the walls. I was magnetically drawn to him, listening with an open mind and heart to every word he spoke.

In the the course of that evening I learned about "Agni Yoga" — a spiritual practice that promised to show me how to heal my life. I was introduced to the secrets of the miraculous, and I was initiated into the basic level of this complex and serious training in inner light-fire.[1]

I did not know then what I know now — that this work, once begun, would be all encompassing, affecting every area of my life. I did not realize that the work of awakening to the spirit within is life-long and that the specialized work of healing would be only a small fraction of what I needed to do.

I was embarking on a journey that would demand risking new experiences, moving from one end of the country to the other, leaving friends and family who no longer supported me. This journey would, in short, demand a willingness on my part to *surrender to the messages of a power greater than who I thought myself to be* — doing whatever I was guided to do, going whenever and wherever I felt inner directed to go.

As it is the nature of light to reveal what is dark, what blocks the full joy of being in the light, some of this transformational journey has felt bleak and unending. As I've patiently and persistently worked at cleansing and purifying my inner psyche — scrubbing the grit and grime that had collected from years of disuse — I've been reborn into light. As I have worked with light-fire to consume what was false to my nature, I have slowly felt the dark clouds that engulfed me open to allow the sun's rays to brighten my journey.

---

[1] Agni means "fire." Agni Yoga is a way of becoming whole through the process of utilizing inner light to literally burn away what is false to the individual — what separates the individual from his or her divine nature. Light-fire is an alchemical agent which transmutes energy held by false conditioned programming, freeing it to express the individual's essence. The techniques described in this book will clarify how this process works.

Through this process my life has changed dramatically. A twenty-year addiction to food has long since disappeared. My work has grown from a boring, meaningless endeavor to a fulfilling, creative expression. And although I once was unable to find and sustain healthy intimate relationships, I am now enjoying a marriage in which feelings and needs are openly expressed and respected. It is a relationship based on mutual creative, emotional and spiritual growth.

Because my own transformation has been so profound, I feel a responsibility to return to the universe the gift that has been given to me. This book is an expression of gratitude to those bearers of light who tread the path before me and who were there as wayshowers — those who took it upon themselves to stand steady in the light of the divine so that I might come to see my own divine nature reflected in their eyes.

ABOUT THIS BOOK

The Healing Power of Inner Light-Fire is an introduction to the powerful teachings that have enabled me to heal my life. Included are a variety of techniques that I've acquired on my journey, but the principal debt, by far, is to the work of Russell Paul Schofield. The school that he founded, Actualism, was formally organized in the early 60s but purposely kept a low profile, relying on word of mouth to attract new students. Consequently, it has escaped the notice of many in the human potential movement. Actualism is dedicated to the teaching of lightwork as a means of personal and planetary transformation and to the process of helping each individual open to his or her own inner source of higher wisdom, love and creativity.

Knowledge of inner light-fire dates back thousands of years and spans cultures across the globe: from Tibetan Buddhists to Hawaiian kahunas, from Chinese Taoists to native American shamans, from medieval alchemists to ancient Egyptian and Persian priests.[1] The New Testament when read more literally than figuratively, seems to indicate that Jesus was also a bearer and teacher of inner light. Throughout the ages, inner light has been seen and verified repeatedly by those with extended sensory perception. That most of us cannot see inner light need not hinder our acceptance of its reality. Our universe is populated by numerous forms of energy — X-

---

[1]Ralph Metzner, *Maps of Consciousness* (New York: Collier Books, 1971), p. 142; and Mary Coddington, *In Search of the Healing Energy* (New York: Destiny Books, 1978), p. 16.

rays, gamma rays, electricity — that cannot be seen by the human eye. In fact, only 2% of the known electromagnetic wave spectrum is visible to us. Indeed, not that long ago the existence of these forms of energy would have been denied because the instrumentation had not yet been developed to document them.

Each person has the capacity to tap into and express his or her own inner source of light. This is true regardless of belief — Buddhist, agnostic, Muslim, Jewish, pagan or any denomination of Christianity. Inner light is part of the actual design of humanity and as such can be used by anyone for healing, growth and transformation.

The lightwork presented herein is a practical method of infusing the individual with the "light of the soul." Light reveals. Light-fire "consumes" in a step-by-step manner what is false to our actual nature, the false conditioning that veils the truth of our being. As we apply ourselves to the purpose of infusing personality with light on a daily basis, we come to express more and more the radiance of our divine nature in our daily lives.

The transformational process can be viewed at three different levels or octaves: as a personal process, as a relationship process and as a planetary process. *The Healing Power of Inner Light-Fire* focuses on the solitary process[2] in which an individual works primarily on the self to heal the wounds and remove the conditioning that blocks the manifestation of higher consciousness.

Some of the techniques described herein are taken directly from the school of Actualism with permission. Others are my adaptations and have been used in workshops and support groups during the past few years with much success.

The book is divided into four parts. Part 1 describes five key truths that form the foundation of

---

[2]Both the relationship and planetary processes as paths of spiritual growth are too immense and too important to be relegated to chapters. As such, this book is the first part of a trilogy covering the three arenas of transformation.

transformation. These truths are not techniques; they are simple axioms that when applied to life never fail to bring you into greater union with higher power. The exercises can be used to help you apply the information to your own life. It is not necessary, however, to do the exercises before going on to Part 2.

Part 2 presents an ordered progression of basic techniques designed to move you away from conditioned programming and into greater alignment with your divine nature. This is achieved by learning how to (1) release from your conditioning, (2) navigate with your awareness into higher consciousness, and (3) tap into and channel light in order to reveal and transform lower states of consciousness. As you read through this part, you can either take time to do the exercises as they appear or mark them and go back to them later. The progression of exercises culminates in the Daily Meditation described on pages 91-92, which is a prerequisite for practicing the techniques described in Parts 3 and 4.

Part 3 discusses the work of personality transformation. You will be shown how to distinguish between and dialogue with the many conditioned and higher aspects of yourself that make up your individuality. You will be shown how to use your basic light tools to free the conditioned parts of yourself from ways of being that block your awareness of and expression of higher power in your daily life. Because the next part deals with a specialized aspect of personality transformation — the inner child — it is necessary for you to read and understand Part 3 before going on to Part 4.

Part 4 deals with the work of healing your past. You will meet your inner child, listen to his or her feelings and special needs and be introduced to a number of exercises for discovering, protecting and reparenting this vital source of inner creativity and love.

Because it will be necessary to have your eyes closed for most of the exercises, I suggest you tape the exercises before doing them or do them in group formation with one member reading the exercise to the others. As an alternative, professional audiocassettes may be purchased from LivingQuest. (See Resources, pp. 151-152.)

Before doing an exercise, seat yourself comfortably in a quiet area of your home with no external distractions. In most of the exercises you will be taking an exploratory inner journey. This is best achieved by closing your eyes and becoming completely relaxed. Begin by breathing into your abdomen. Experience as the breath moves on up into your diaphragm and upper chest. Think of releasing tension as you exhale slowly. Continue inhaling and exhaling slowly. When you are totally relaxed, proceed with the exercise.

If while trying to do an exercise you experience "nothing," it is possible that you are working against a defense structure of denial that is serving to protect you from pain. If this is so, I have found that pushing the work accomplishes little. You might ask your higher self for guidance or do the simple Downpour with Light (pp. 81-82) and ask that the defenses be released at the best timing for the whole of your personality. I have found that it is possible to get results from this work even when not experiencing much directly. Just think of the light and let yourself relax and trust the process.

Upon finishing an exercise, slowly open your eyes and come back into the room. Allow yourself time (at least ten to fifteen minutes) to assimilate your experience and ground yourself before continuing with your daily activities. You may want to have a cup of tea or do some gentle stretching.

For optimal benefit, the exercises should be done regularly. I would suggest doing the Daily Meditation at the beginning of each day to raise your consciousness and set the tone for your daily activities. As you proceed throughout your day, be aware of particular events and people who affect your state of consciousness. When you have time later, you can use these events and states of consciousness to fuel the deeper work of personality transformation. Many of the exercises are geared to bring up deep unresolved issues so that they may be healed. In these instances and in cases where unresolved childhood issues cannot be healed or completed in one sitting, it is crucial to allow yourself at least an hour of assimilation and adjustment. In fact, I suggest you do the transformational work (outlined in Parts 3 and 4) in the evening after your daily activities and commitments are over. In order to initiate and maintain major life change, the work you do must be searching, disciplined and ongoing. In working with light-fire, obstructions to well-being are revealed and peeled away step by step, layer by layer.

If you are seriously interested in this transformational process, I recommend you eventually find a teacher with whom to work. The techniques presented here are powerful, but basic. There are many more finely tuned methods to deepen inner healing. (See Resources, pp. 151-152, for specific ways to follow up on this suggestion.)

Throughout the years I have come across various books, practitioners and institutes which have utilized light in some manner, usually metaphorically, but I have never encountered anything else that approaches the breadth, depth, power and vision of the tools and techniques that I have experienced. Inner light-fire is one of our creator's ultimate gifts to humanity. It is neither a concept nor a flight of imagination; it is a living reality. I hope to give you a more detailed understanding and experience of the profound treasure that each of us carries within.

PART ONE

KEYS TO ACCESSING HIGHER POWER

It is midnight, Friday, September 13, 1985. On vacation in Durango, Colorado, we have just begun our last weekend of adventure as a child-free married couple. I am seven months pregnant. These next few days are to be a ritual signifying the closure of this time of our lives. "When we get back to Dallas," Gene says, "we'll get serious about childbirth preparation." "Yup," I agree with him as I head toward the bathroom.

My bedtime preparation is just about complete when I notice some liquid gushing from between my legs. "What's this?" I think to myself but say nothing. And then some more liquid, this time drowning my underwear and nightgown. "Something's not right!" I'm alarmed now. With the third gush I begin frantically pulling a towel from the motel shelf and stuffing it between my legs.

"Gene," I yell, "I think my water broke. I think we're having our baby." My mind is furiously trying to compute the whole thing. "Go get help. Wake the motel owners up. Ask them where the hospital is!" I am panicking. Only seven months pregnant; only an eleven pound gain. "Is there even a baby in there?" I've no idea. I've never done this before.

Within minutes Gene is back, panting. "No one answers. No one's there. Let's just get in the car. Something's got to be open somewhere." It is dark. We drive. Nothing. Neither of us knows which direction to go in. I am praying. "Dear God, please let this baby be okay." We go left. Then right. Darkness. Nothing. My eyes search the street for some sign of life. And then I see a sign. "Gene, there, to the left. It says 'Hospital'". "Thank God," I think as we hurriedly rush inside the most welcome emergency room I've ever set eyes on.

The hours that follow are the most frightening time of my life. As my contractions begin to appear, I can no longer pretend this is not truly happening. The doctors have determined the fetus is breathing. The heartbeat is good. "But," they say, "there's only a 40% chance your baby will be healthy. You have to decide within the hour if you wish to be flown by air ambulance to Albuquerque. We don't have the intensive care facilities to handle a premature lung condition. If the baby's born in critical condition, we will have to fly you both out and that'll be more stress on the baby's condition. Let us know what you decide to do. "

I sob. It all seems too much. But I know I am going to have to get a grip on myself and come to a clear place of wisdom. If ever I needed my lightwork training, it is now. I take some deep breaths. I try to stay relaxed. My contractions are coming about five minutes apart. More and more of my energy is going into the labor. Less and less is available for anything else. I look at Gene. "What are we going to do?" I close my eyes and feel into my pain. It is fear. All of it is fear. I hold the fear in the light and I pray for clarity.

I look around me. This place is comforting. The nurses are friendly and I feel a sense of trust. My contractions are taking more out of me. I have no more energy for anything except the business at hand — giving birth. I look at Gene and I know he feels the same. It is as if this is where we were meant to be and our child was meant to be born.

I let the silence within myself deepen. I hold the fear and confusion in inner fire. I feel at peace and I know without a doubt that our baby will be okay. With the serenity of inner security, I labor my first child into the world — a healthy 4 lb. 6 oz. baby boy.

It is one of the most difficult things to do at times — to trust higher power. And yet every time I do I am awed at the perfection of life's plan. The lesson of trust is simple. It calls for full awareness of pain and a willingness to surrender it to higher power. It demands we let go of attachments to outcome, living in the flow of life as it is presented. It demands we open to the guidance available to us from higher knowing and that we act decisively on this guidance. There is no room for fear, confusion or doubt. If we are to live in the center of our power, we must walk in the world as a warrior — with willingness and determination to stand steady in the light of higher consciousness.)

PAIN

"Goddamn it, Lisa, stop the practicing now!" The drumming continues a few yards from the dining room table. I cringe. Here we go again. Immersed in the rat-a-tat-tat of sticks on drums, she is oblivious to the desperate demands of our father, who wishes only to eat his dinner in peace. Mom cries. I sit there helpless. Those sounds pierce my ears, too. "Which is worse?" I wonder, "the drums, the yelling or the crying?"

Dad bolts upright, throws his napkin down and storms about. Lisa refuses to budge. Now the obstinate expression on her face is more apparent. If it could speak it would say, "Hey! You screwed up — so take this!" One punch, then another punch — BANG, POW, BANG as the sticks hit the drum.

My mom and dad were victims of a society in which anger, rage, emptiness and grief are buried under facades of glamor and perfection. Society teaches us how to "succeed," not how to listen to the feelings of our children. Like so many other kids, my growing pains were ignored. My parents just didn't know how to listen. If I was angry or upset, Mom felt guilty and became defensive. So I gave up. So, it seemed to me, did Lisa. She used her drums to yell and scream. I used overeating. I also used school to drown my feelings by getting and maintaining high grades. With "A's," I got the strokes I so badly needed. When I left home, I turned my sights towards successful men and glamorous jobs, at the

What is success to you 3 to 5 yrs from now? Good interview question!

expense of my feelings and true needs. The pain of not
being heard stayed with me, bubbling just below the
surface, then erupting time after time, like a volcano,
destroying everything in its path.

For years I looked to food, men, money and success
to ease my inner turmoil. But I learned that if I ran from
my pain, seeking refuge in glamor, parties, work, money
or sex, my monsters reared their ugly heads in more
horrible ways. I ultimately discovered that no person or
thing could patch me up and make me whole. The only
way I could permanently fill this inner void was by
meeting it head on — traveling inwardly to its ugly
beginnings, unraveling its personal meaning for me and
gently, oh so gently, embracing its hidden wisdom and
love. When I closed my eyes and went "within" — into
the dark recesses of my heart and mind — and lifted the
darkness, or filled the infinite emptiness with light, or
spoke to it and listened to what it had to say, I began to
change. As I wrestled with my monsters and eventually
learned to embrace their infinite grace, a higher power
slowly began to manifest in my life.

Pain is the gauge that indicates there is an aspect of
life that needs attention — that requires us to let go, to
move forward, to take a risk, to make a "shift in
consciousness." Pain is fuel — a form of energy to be
experienced and transformed by the ever-evolving
organism. Our task is to discover what the stagnant,
blocked, stillborn areas of our lives are and to begin a
process of opening, digesting, assimilating and releasing.

Yet we are born into a culture that goes to great
lengths to stop pain as quickly and conveniently as
possible. Few of us are ever encouraged to sit with our
pain. More often, the prevailing advice is to cover it up,
deaden it, leave it behind. We sit glazed in front of the
TV watching the fantasy lives of others, ignoring the
inner depths of our own. Millions consume aspirin,
Tylenol or Valium as a daily staple. Many of us in recent
generations were born into this world drugged.

Frequently, we are numb to the birth of our own children. We often leave life drugged as well. Most of us miss all the major life events because our senses are dulled in an attempt to avoid pain.

We have inherited a world view that does not encourage us to look behind the surface of issues. Our official medicine treats the symptoms of disease while generally ignoring the more demanding search for underlying causes. Television hypnotizes us with a parade of visual and sound "bites" — all show and little substance. Unlike traditional cultures, we have created virtually no meaningful initiations or rites of passage that penetrate appearances and address our actual needs: personal growth and evolution. Instead, we've created what no traditional culture ever had: an almost universally addicted and/or alienated population, ceaselessly anesthetizing and diverting itself with external substances and activities. We constantly strive to erect and maintain our own "Great Wall" against the void within us. We beat back unwanted feelings and memories, pain and stress, slaying them with alcohol, drugs, food, sex or whatever works.

I'm not advocating throwing away all our painkillers, but I think the practice has become too indiscriminate. It is one thing to numb the pain of drilled teeth, surgery or terminal cancer. It is another to run to the liquor cabinet at the first sign of loneliness, or to food at the first sign of anger, or to TV as a way to numb the gnawing discontent with our lives.

This automatic, conditioned avoidance of pain — *without comprehending its message* — exacts a heavy cost. We need to discover the meaning of the pain in our lives. As we open to the inner message of our pain — embracing it — we discover and reclaim aspects of ourselves that we badly need. All the while I was compulsively overeating there was a little girl inside of me calling for help. "Love me," she'd whisper in my ear as I reached for the ice cream in the freezer. I didn't hear her because I wasn't looking for her. I didn't know there was a message hidden within this addiction because no one had ever alerted me to this fact.) We all want the same simple things: to love and be loved, to play and create, to build confidence and power. Pain is the great motivator, the initiator of all fundamental change. If we heed its message, we are born anew. If we don't, we become the victims of stagnation, destined to repeat the same patterns that created the pain in the first place.

Avoid pain and it grows. Listen to it and you grow.

Exercise: Discovering the Meaning of Pain

In what ways do you distract yourself from pain? Do you use relationships, drink, drugs, sex, TV, food or work to avoid your own emptiness? Become aware of the areas in your life that cause discomfort. How might the pain evoked by these situations motivate you to change?

Close your eyes. Become deeply relaxed. Move with your awareness into the silent center of yourself. Now visualize yourself in a painful situation. Ask yourself what the hidden lesson here is for you. What might you need to learn from this situation, to be free of its pain forever? Remain quiet and listen.

ATTACHMENT

For many years I clamored after prestige. I believed that if I were given a chance, I would become a great video director. I went at it with all I had. The jobs I secured were stressful and often boring. I was overworked and underpaid. But I held on tenaciously to the belief that once I'd paid my dues, I would graduate into the big time, attain the glorious fruits of this exciting profession and the subsequent happiness that this achievement would bring. These fantasies drove me, but my day-to-day experience continued to leave me exhausted and stressed out. My goal of excitement, glamor and prestige was never attained. Blaming the profession for its inability to give me what I wanted, I turned my sights elsewhere.

Similarly, in relationships I looked to men who were successful in their chosen fields. In college I had affairs with two married professors. It didn't matter that they were not emotionally available for me. What mattered was that they appeared to have what I wanted — recognition and prestige. Later I became involved with a very wealthy and acclaimed artist. He had it "all," and I thought that if I attached myself to him, I would vicariously have it all, too. Neither of us was remotely capable of love at that time, and when we inevitably broke up (after three years!), I became desperately aware of my own internal emptiness.

I tried to fill that emptiness with food, with more men and with fantasies of fame. I became obsessed with work, stopping at nothing to achieve what I thought

31

would get me to the top. Becoming sexually involved with one of my employers seemed to be one of the requirements for making it. I worked for slave wages, sixteen hours a day, for the privilege of sleeping with another unavailable married man. All the while I avoided looking at the source of my unhappiness. Something in me knew that things weren't right, but I had no models, no guidelines for even beginning to discover what was wrong. Again and again I did what everyone else seemed to do — I turned to things outside of myself to make me feel better.

(This tendency to look outside ourselves for solutions, mood alteration and personal validation is what I call attachment. Being born into a fundamentally materialistic culture instills a reliance on externals to ease our pain, to give ourselves emotional boosts, to make ourselves feel worthwhile, sexy, smart and powerful. Underlying all attachment is a felt void or emptiness. We try to fill that emptiness by turning outward to others, to things and to events. Each of us thinks, "I must have this, be this, do this, feel this, think this, in order to feel okay about me." We struggle to make circumstances fit our desires and needs.)

The problem with this approach is that we cannot control things outside of ourselves. We cannot make someone love us. We cannot make our boss give us a raise. We cannot make our children call us or send us birthday cards. And when the things that we are attached to do not work out the way we hoped, we are thrown back into the emptiness which is at the core of all attachment. We may then turn to alcohol, drugs, food, work or sex to ease the pain. But always, without fail, the effects of these substances wear off — we must then indulge in them again to keep the pain away.

"But what about healthy attachment?" some of you might be asking. "What about being involved in life?" Many of us confuse attachment with involvement. They are not the same thing. Attachment is being stuck in an involvement and arises from a fear of letting go. Being involved yet detached enables us to immerse ourselves totally in the circumstances of life while remaining flexible. This gives us the ability to move fluidly in and out of the events of our lives — as they change.

Loving deeply yet being able to let go of the object of our love when needs change is an example of involved detachment. Clinging to the object of our love even when we realize that person can no longer give us what we need is an example of attachment. Attachment comes from an inability to accept change, an inability to move with the flow of life. An attachment forms when the mind thinks it needs to have something that isn't there.

"But I'm all alone and I know an intimate relationship would make me happier. Isn't it healthier to be in a good relationship? Shouldn't I strive for this in my life?" You bet! But there is a difference between having goals and dramatizing lacks. Attachment creates a desperate need to be in a relationship and causes us to feel inadequate without it. Being detached allows us to accept the beauty inherent in being alone while preparing ourselves for greater intimacy. Detachment acknowledges the temporality of all things.

To cultivate detachment in our culture is difficult because we are conditioned to live for the future — to strive for beauty, glamor, popularity, wealth and success. We are programmed to believe these things will bring happiness. We operate with the expectation that achieving these things is what life is about — the ultimate panacea. And so we race about trying to achieve and we think, "When I'm thin . . . When I'm wealthy . . . When I'm successful . . . then I'll be happy!"

It doesn't work that way. I know. I've been there. And I've discovered that being thin won't fill the hole inside, being wealthy and successful won't fill the emptiness, even being loved won't do it. Why? Because emptiness is what we feel when we are separated from our source. Ancient Chinese philosophers espoused living in the Tao, the mystical flow of life, by fully accepting what is. (Reconnecting with the flow of life is the only way to fill the hole inside, a hole that has in part been created by a society that teaches people that happiness is always around the next bend — when we get that promotion, build our dream house, lose ten pounds.

Being attached in this way — to specific things to make us happy — is in fact the cause of our suffering. When we fixate on something that isn't, we miss what is! It is the conflict between what we *think we need* (our attachments) and what *is* that creates our suffering. We may suffer from the conflict between an attachment to having the perfect body and our actual body size.) We may suffer from the conflict between an attachment to another's love and his or her actual inability to express love. We may suffer from the conflict between an attachment to the achievement of a specific goal and the reality that the goal is unattained. All of these attachments, conflicting with reality, cause suffering.

(When we fully let ourselves be with what is, with the way it is unfolding, our capacity to enjoy life greatly expands. The conflict resolves itself and suffering ceases. Because most suffering can be expressed as the conflict between the way things are and the way we think we need them to be, it follows that if we want to alleviate our suffering, we must resolve our conflicts. As it is impossible to change what is already happening, the only two ways I know of to resolve conflict are to change what will be and/or to change our attachments.

Control is not the way to change what will be. It is an artificial attempt to contain or force energy to go in a direction it does not intend to go.) How much success have you had in making someone love you or act the way you want him or her to act? Trying to get someone to love you is a futile task. You can expend enormous amounts of energy trying to manipulate love. You may hide your differences, thinking that if you are the same as the other person, he or she will love you. You may cater

34

to another's needs at the expense of your own, thinking that if you sacrifice yourself, you will gain love. You may cry and throw tantrums, thinking that you can make the other person feel guilty enough to love you. Although you may try your damnedest to make that person feel and be something that he or she isn't, you fail. Most of us who have tried to change our lives in this way — attempting to control, manipulate, make others and events be the way we want them to be — suffer the consequences of repetitive failure.

Life has its own processes. It unfolds in its own way and time. This is the Tao. When we try to intervene and make events or processes happen differently, even if we are "successful," more often than not the process reinstates itself with even more force and determination. Anyone who has tried to stop eating, drinking or doing drugs by using willpower knows it rarely works. Witness the many people who diet and lose weight, only to quickly resume their out-of-control eating patterns when control has been slackened. Although these methods can work temporarily, they rarely last because "controlling" is a very ineffective way to permanently change anything. We may use it successfully at times to break destructive habit patterns, but, ultimately, permanent change must come from within.

When we align with higher power (as described in Parts 2, 3 and 4), becoming a co-creator, we can use the power of thought to assist in the creation of our destiny. Conflicts resolve themselves because the joy and love felt in unifying with the presence of this power overcome the small desires and needs of the personality; we become so deeply fulfilled that the need for the objects of our attachments disappears. Our suffering ceases as this conflict is resolved. From this perspective we see the "actual design" of the true self. Our will becomes aligned with a greater will, and we think and act in alignment with the power that maintains and sustains all of life.

The second way to resolve the pain that comes from conflict is to drop our attachments and expectations of outcome. (This is achieved by disidentifying with our conditioning and aligning with our nonjudgmental observer and/or higher self. How to do this is discussed in Parts 2 and 3.) In so doing, we automatically open to what is. We surrender our personality's desire for things, people and events to be a certain way. In surrendering these expectations, we allow ourselves to be in life as it is. We totally accept and embrace who we are and what is happening. Because we have stopped fighting life, we open to a peace and serenity never before imagined.

When you become aware that you are forming an attachment, let it go. Look within to the source of your unhappiness. Go into the pain. Explore it. Embrace it. Uplift it. Reconnect with the Tao, with life, with the source.

Exercise: Discovering Your Attachments

Make a list of the things you believe will bring you greater happiness or fulfillment. Often, this is a three-step process. For example, you may believe, "When I have more money, I will be more powerful and this will make me happy." Or, "When I am thinner, I'll be more successful (or popular) and then I'll be happy." Fill in the blanks below:

When I have ___, I'll be ___ and then I'll be ____.
When I am ____, I'll be ____ and then I'll be ____.

CONSCIOUSNESS

In the summer between my sophomore and junior years of college, the cockroaches and I shared a torn-up mattress on the floor of an old tenement building in New York City. A few years later I rented an old, filthy pork factory with enough space to live and sculpt but with inadequate heat and no kitchen. When I moved in I painted the walls black and turned the men's urinal into my shower. I stayed there for seven years!

Through all of this, I used my environment as a primary excuse for my misery. To cover up my feelings of unworthiness, I maintained the belief that in order to be happy I needed to move to the mountains. Notice the attachment here? My teachers told me again and again that I could experience happiness within myself. But I refused to make the necessary shifts in consciousness. I preferred to stay stuck in scarcity and deprivation.

Years later, when my husband and I moved to Dallas, our first apartment was located on a major thoroughfare with a seemingly endless stretch of MacDonald's, Arby's, Burger King, Wendy's. No trees. No grass. No place to walk. No mountains. Lots of supermarkets. I had never seen so many supermarkets!

I sobbed myself to sleep every night for the first six months. "Let's leave," I cried to Gene, knowing full well we couldn't. I wanted out so badly, but there was nowhere to go. The nearest mountains were an eight-hour drive away in Arkansas. I was stuck.

I wallowed in self-pity, crying to my teachers to help me out of my misery. They said, "You have the beauty within — and you have the choice and the tools to access it." But I was stubborn. I refused to look at and let go of the pain. Things weren't changing. They weren't getting any better.

That fall, Gene and I took a trip to the mountains outside of Colorado Springs. As I walked among the yellow aspen, my mind ran its negative messages again and again while my eyes explored the beauty before me. Even my obsessing could not keep me from sensing the inner beauty that was being reflected back to me. While praying to understand and be guided out of my misery, I suddenly reconnected with a lost sense of power. I knew that I did not deserve to live the way I had been living and that I would do whatever I needed to do not to live that way again.

On returning to Dallas, I immediately shifted my focus. I became passionately involved in exploring this power — letting go of ideas I had had about what I should be doing — and doing instead what inspired me with vision. Suddenly it didn't really matter where I lived because I felt creatively alive.

Sure, I had my moments — like when I had to wade through the carbon monoxide exhaust of bumper-to-bumper cars caught in rush hour traffic on the freeway under construction near our apartment. Or when the airport (only ten miles from our apartment complex) routed airplanes in and out over our heads, the noise rumbling through my solar plexus every few minutes. Sure, I hated it! But using my light tools, I began consciously working to open to higher power by releasing self-pity and negativity. Let loose from negative conditioning, I began aligning with this power. Soon new opportunities presented themselves. We found a home with a big backyard and a rooster next door. The neighborhood had only one supermarket, no freeway and no airport. This was perhaps the first time in my life I actually felt at peace with my environment.

This serenity lasted a year. And then I was challenged. Our family was expanding and our house began to feel too small. I found myself becoming irritated and angry. At first I gave in to this negativity and found myself obsessing about what we didn't have. But still determined to maintain alignment with higher power, I again used my light tools to free myself of negative consciousness, magnifying my gratitude for what we did have.

Then Gene lost his job! At first I panicked. How much money did we have? What were we going to do? We talked, exploring our options. By the end we both understood that this was the opportunity we'd been waiting for — the chance to leave. Nothing held us here now. We were free!

Within two months we were on our way to Boulder, Colorado. My fantasies of mountain living were about to become a reality, and I knew I had done it! I had remained firm in the belief that I could change my reality to reflect my higher sense of power. I had transformed the negative consciousness that blocked this power and I had stayed centered in the love and light of this power's consciousness.

(The years I spent living in places I didn't really want to be taught me some lessons — the long, hard way. First, I learned to be aware of and sensitive to the minute-to-minute experience of living. Was I enjoying it? Or was I irritable, stressed, angry? What was my state of consciousness? That was a major part of the lesson — to become aware of and heed the "state of consciousness" I was in on a minute-to-minute basis. Second, I learned that no matter what outer action I took to change my quality of life, if I did not address the state of consciousness I was in, the quality of my life would not change. In order to make the outer change I first had to change the state of consciousness I was in.) This awareness was the beginning of leaving behind a life of unfulfillment for one which brings richness and joy.

(A state of consciousness is a total mental-feeling-perceiving way of being.) Many spiritual disciplines distinguish between low-frequency and high-frequency states of consciousness. As a rule, a low-frequency state

39

of consciousness is felt as a "negative" experience that tends to drag us down. Low frequency disempowers us, generally causing us to feel separate from others, humanity and a higher power. Examples of low frequency are fear, hate, rage, anger, guilt, grief, ill-will, confusion, idealization, rigidity and judgmentalism.

A high-frequency state of consciousness is felt as a "positive" experience that tends to uplift us. High frequency empowers us and causes us to feel connected with others, humanity and a higher power. Examples of high frequency are joy, peace, love, forgiveness, compassion, clarity, wisdom, flexibility, acceptance and openness.

The states of consciousness we find ourselves in attract to us people and events that are in similar states of consciousness. For example, if we hold onto a lot of anger (consciously or unconsciously) and project that anger outwardly onto others, we will for the most part attract angry people into our lives or people who make us even angrier. If, on the other hand, we emanate joy and love, most people and situations in our lives will reflect that high-frequency state of consciousness back to us.

For the purpose of being able to bring more happiness and fulfillment into our lives, it is imperative we find a way to move out of low-frequency states of consciousness and live in high-frequency states of consciousness *most of the time.* If we try to create more happiness in our lives by looking outside of ourselves, we are missing the point. Unhappiness is a consciousness state. So is happiness. The most effective way to become happy is to learn how to *shift* out of a state of unhappiness into a state of happiness. That is the most direct, powerful and permanent way to change our experience of reality.

In order to truly master this, we must learn how to alter our inner state of consciousness at *will.* We do this by fully experiencing and moving through lower consciousness so that we may embrace and discover the wisdom held within. (How to do this is discussed in

Part 3.) (WARNING: It is not uncommon to want to side step the pain and move into the appearance of high-frequency. In fact, it is common for many "seekers" of truth to hold an "idealized" idea of spirituality and to try to live that ideal by avoiding or denying the darker sides of the self. No true spiritual growth can occur without acknowledging and moving through the darkness for it is the darkness that holds the hidden key to enlightenment. "Idealization" is a form of low-frequency consciousness that has the appearance of high-frequency. It may take the form of pseudo love, pseudo high, pseudo inspiration, pseudo caring. Some common examples are the person who gives in order to be liked or approved of; the person who is the "life of the party" because he or she can't deal with real feeling; or the person who maintains an appearance of centeredness in order to feel spiritually superior.

In order to grow we must make the shift out of low-frequency by moving into and through the low-frequency first. If we are caught in an idealized state of consciousness, we must ask, "What is the motive for needing to appear different than I am? Why the need to pretend? What real feelings am I avoiding?")

When we work regularly to move through our pain in order to uplift our states of consciousness, LIFE DOES NOT STAY THE SAME. When we shift out of a state of helplessness, we no longer meet the needs of abusive partners. When we begin to love ourselves, our bodies express the beauty of our inner essence. And when we open to experience the joy of each moment, new opportunities for creativity and advancement in our work come our way.

Human beings are consciousness systems. Gaining mastery over your consciousness gains you mastery over your life.

Exercise: Awareness of States of Consciousness

What state of consciousness do you generally find yourself in? Are you most often bored, angry, depressed, irritated, worried, or do you usually feel joy, love, excitement and inspiration. How do low-frequency states of consciousness attract low-frequency circumstances and people into your life? Stop at moments throughout the day to become aware of what state of consciousness you are in. Is this a state you want to be in? How would your life change if you could alter this state of consciousness at will?

ENLIGHTENED ACTION

For many years I did work that felt meaningless and unnurturing of my creativity. I put in eight hours of drudgery every day, five days a week, working for temporary agencies, earning $5-7 an hour, which was hardly my idea of prosperity! The agencies sent me on jobs which I had to do once I had made the commitment. I hit bottom when I was sent on a secretarial job to IBM. Although I knew how to lift my state of consciousness, I chose to stay depressed. I was afraid that if I let myself feel good, I'd never leave. I'd be doomed to stay at IBM for the rest of my life. Well, as long as I refused to uplift my state of consciousness, I stayed right there at IBM. It wasn't until I began to work to lift out of my hopelessness and despair that I encountered new opportunity.

While feeling good one day, I spotted a new computer in the office. No one was around and there was no work to do. I wasn't feeling sorry for myself, so my thoughts and feelings were clear. Noticing a manual, I began to read and before I knew it was well into teaching myself a new word processing system. By the end of the week I was on the phone to my employment agency. "How much can I earn doing Displaywriter?" I asked. "Eight to ten dollars an hour" was the reply. "Send me out," I said. "I've just taught myself." That next week I was out of IBM forever. Sure, I was still doing temporary work, but I was challenged by the new computer system, *and* I was earning $3 more an hour.

It wasn't long before I had gained enough skill and experience to risk a bigger step. I wrote letters to fifteen law firms which used the new system I had learned describing my skills and experience. Within three weeks I was hired as a free-lance word processing operator, earning $15 an hour, forty hours a week. Not bad for a person who was earning less than half as much only a few months before. The job lasted a couple of years. Not only was I making more money than I had ever made, I also liked the people I worked with and eventually had extraordinary flexibility with my hours during a pregnancy and child-rearing phase.

When in higher consciousness it is imperative we learn to listen to inner direction and follow through with decisive action. If we do not, we have not earned the right to manifest higher consciousness. *Experiencing* higher consciousness and *manifesting* a life that reflects higher consciousness are two separate things.

In the preceding example, yes, I had made the shift out of despair, but it was my ability to recognize and follow through with new opportunity that changed my life. I could have ignored the manual in my office, preferring to use the time to gossip with co-workers. I could have been too frightened and insecure to risk calling my agency, and I could have thought to myself, "Others may be worth $15 an hour — not me." Then I would have stayed right where I was.

One of my clients has ongoing relationship problems. When she comes to work with me, we work to lift the sadness in her heart area. When she leaves, she feels good and knows exactly what changes she needs to make. She rarely follows through, however, keeping the same unfulfilling relationships in her life despite her own higher knowing to let go. They drag her down and use up her energy. Then she's back again to work on lifting the same sadness.

All change involves risk. Whenever we move forward into the unknown, we risk losing what we had before. If we are afraid to risk, we are afraid to lose that which we are attached to. This kind of fear is a low-frequency state of consciousness, and it perpetuates low-frequency states of consciousness in our lives. In order to maintain higher consciousness, we must shift out of fear. It is only when we free ourselves sufficiently of lower states of consciousness (including fear) so that we may *follow through with enlightened action* that we are able to maintain the changed lifestyle higher consciousness brings.

When you make inner shifts in consciousness, you are usually tested — perhaps once, twice, even three times. These tests are challenges to "stand steady" in higher consciousness despite circumstances or events which have had the power in the past to pull you down. If, for example, you have tended to be judgmental and have been releas this form of low frequency, you may find yourself challenged by things that used to trigger your judgmental attitudes — your boss writes illegible notes to you, your best friend marries a "jerk" or your sister forgets your birthday. When you are able to stand steady within the higher consciousness of compassion despite these events, you will be given some form of inner direction in combination with a new opportunity. You may be inner guided to make amends to those you've hurt in the past, or to let go of relationships that no longer serve you. When you act in response to higher prompting, you will be ushered into more and more of the goodness of life. Your compassion may come back to you in the form of deeper relationships, gifts of caring or even greater financial reward. Again, if you do not act as your inner guidance directs, you will lose the opportunity to experience greater goodness. This opportunity will be lost until you are ready and willing to take action.

Fortunately, circumstances and events always mirror our present state of consciousness. In this way, you can simply use the process of your life to determine what changes need to be made to further your growth. If you never seem to have enough money, then use this situation to determine what state of consciousness is creating your survival income level. When you make a shift in consciousness, new opportunities will present themselves. When you release the low-frequency perception, "I don't deserve an abundant life," an opportunity for promotion or investment may present itself. If you have sufficiently enlightened the consciousness surrounding this area, you will embrace this new opportunity. If you are still partly affected by lower consciousness (fear of financial loss or fear of increased responsibility, for example), you will pass up the opportunity until you are ready to make the shift. Your challenge is to discover the states of consciousness that prevent you from moving forward. If you fail to act decisively, your challenge is to discover why and change it.

**To sustain higher consciousness
you must recognize opportunities for change,
listen to higher direction and
follow through with right action.**

Exercise: Discovering Fear of Risk

If after moving into higher states of consciousness, you continually put yourself in situations or environments that have negative effects, ask yourself, "Why won't I make the choice to change my situation? What benefit do I derive from repeating this old behavior? What am I afraid of risking?" Then use the techniques described in Parts 2, 3 and 4 to release these fears.

WILL

"I feel so lousy. Please, help me!" I
can't count the number of times I said something like this
in my life. I loved thinking I was powerless. It gave me
an excuse to stay a little girl. I didn't want to grow up
and take responsibility for myself or my life. I didn't
want to take responsibility because I was afraid I would
fail. If it was no one else's fault that my life was so
lousy, it'd have to be mine, wouldn't it? Unconsciously,
I pretended I was helpless in order to save face. What I
didn't know then was that no one was responsible for my
life but me — even when I pretended otherwise.
Pretending didn't change the truth.

We all have free will. With each of life's decisions
we are free to choose the action to take or not to take, the
way to be or not to be. Until we become awakened to
our higher nature, much of what we choose is motivated
by fear. Choosing to lose weight may be motivated by a
fear of emotional rejection or possible heart attack.
Choosing a career in law over a career as an artist may be
motivated by fear of financial insecurity or parental
scorn. Choosing to go to graduate school may be
motivated by fear of failure in the world. Wherever there
is fear, an obstruction to higher consciousness is
manifesting in our lives. Actions and behaviors
motivated by fear create for us a life that is out of
alignment with higher power. Whenever we are out of
alignment, we experience struggle.

Willpower is the attempt of the personality to override our fear and make things better through manipulation and control. We attempt to lose weight by depriving our bodies of calories and nutrients. We force ourselves to study law despite our lack of interest. We struggle with our graduate studies despite our desire to be at home with our children. As long as we try to change by exerting willpower, we increase our struggle. Trying to figure things out "logically" or to force ourselves to feel, think or be different than we are is willpower in action. In order to move into higher consciousness, we must be *willing* to change. Will moves our awareness into the center of that which blocks change. Willpower, on the other hand, keeps us stuck in low-frequency states by avoiding that which blocks change. In order to change we must be *willing* to act decisively to move into and embrace our pain, discover the truth held within it and act on our highest wisdom.

No one can do to this for us. No one can make us change. No one can take away our pain. Those who try are doing us a disservice by robbing us of the lessons and messages hidden within the pain. They rob us of our own power. The only way to lift our pain permanently is to do it ourselves. I remember many times, while feeling lousy and out of control, making the choice to sit down, close my eyes and consciously embark on a journey into the pain. I remember choosing to change a negative thought to a positive one. I remember choosing, in spite of the inertia, to "get off my bullshit." Everytime I did, my life got miraculously better. And I learned that if I did not choose to make the shift, I always paid the price.

When you find yourself stuck in low-frequency states of consciousness, ask, "How do I benefit from this?" Not until the benefits of change outweigh the benefits of staying stuck will you find the courage to risk the minideaths that are necessary steps to being reborn into a new self.

The desire to change demands the
***willingness* to do the work of changing.**
No one else can do it for you.

Exercise: Discovering Why You Are Stuck

What low-frequency states of consciousness are you stuck in? Are you using willpower to avoid exploring the consciousness that keeps you stuck? How do you benefit from these low-frequency states of consciousness? What will you lose by moving into higher frequency? Security? Comfort? Familiarity? Approval by family? Others? What are you afraid of achieving? More responsibility? Exposure? Power? Success? Happiness? What would achieving these things mean to your life?

PART TWO

BASIC TECHNIQUES

Russell greets me with a big kiss and has me lie down on the massage table. He is a short, stocky ball of fiery energy. No telling what his age. Rumor has it he is over 150 years old and there is something so ancient about him that the rumor seems plausible. He moves behind me and touches the top of my head. I instantly become a live wire as high intensity light-energy shoots through my body and out the bottoms of my feet. Without any prior knowledge of my life, Russell says, "Jane, you've been ill and on the brink of death. You've been wanting to leave here, but, no matter . . . you've found the light. You will be safe now." My body vibrates at a frequency I never before knew was possible. I have found the light and I know I will stay.

WHAT IS KEEPING YOU STUCK?

Until we make the choice to detach from conditioning and align personality with the higher power of the universe, we respond to our external environments as we have been conditioned to do. Our thoughts, emotions, perceptions and behaviors are determined by our upbringing. No one wakes up in the morning and says, "Today, I'm going to yell at my children and forget my afternoon appointment." No one consciously chooses to neglect or abuse. No one consciously chooses to be worried, afraid, depressed or angry. I certainly never chose to wake up in the middle of the night, every night for nearly ten years, to stuff myself with food. Nevertheless, I did it anyway. I believed I acted the way I did because that was who I was. I was identified with my conditioning. To be identified with conditioning is normal. It simply means we believe the way we have been conditioned to be is truly who we are.

For most of my adult life I identified with being a compulsive overeater. I experienced cravings for food at all hours of the day and night. My mind was obsessed with thoughts of food, with ways to diet and control my eating, with calorie counting and how much I weighed.

I also identified with many debilitating emotional states. I was depressed, fearful and angry. The whole of my identity was enmeshed with these specific aspects of myself. I lost my ability to distinguish between anger and me, fear and me, depression and me. Because I could not distinguish between who I was and how I felt and acted, I was powerless to change any of it. I was stuck in being the way I was conditioned to be.[1]

I was not unusual.

Most of us are stuck in this way. Each of us has programming which gets in the way of ultimate happiness and fulfillment. Each and every one of us is "identified" with particular ways of thinking, feeling, perceiving and acting. That is, we believe the way we think, feel, perceive and act is who we are. Because we are programmed to be the way we are, it is very difficult to change — unless we know how to disengage the program that keeps us identified with our conditioning.

(Much has been written about using positive affirmation and visualization to change this programming. These are powerful and viable tools for change. The shortcoming, however, is that until we have disengaged from our programming, we run the risk of feeding a similar look-alike program into our brain to take its place. The visualizations and positive affirmations we choose may be shaped by our conditioning. For example, if you are conditioned to believe that wealth buys happiness, you may do daily visualizations to improve your financial position within your present career. What if the career you are now in does not reflect your special talents? Visualizing success in this area may bring you that aspect

---

[1]Not all conditioning is bad. Much of the conditioning that forms our personality serves us well. But the fact remains that we rarely make the choice to identify with either "good" or "bad" conditioning, and there may come a time in our lives when the conditioning no longer serves us — when we want to let it go. For example, those of us who come from dysfunctional families are "survivors." We've learned to cope with less than ideal environments in the best way we could. Being the "nice guy" or "good girl" may have gotten us smiling nods from those we most needed and loved but may not be appropriate on our jobs. Being assertive may have won us certain favors in school and at home, but learning to be more yielding and flexible may be necessary in our intimate relationships. As you progress through the exercises in this part, you will learn how to recognize and detach from the conditioning that motivates you. From this detached perspective you may then choose whether you wish to keep or release that aspect of yourself within a specific situational context.

of success, but not fulfillment. Fulfillment comes when you express your unique gifts. Until you release the conditioning that is responsible for your less than optimal career, no amount of visualization will bring you deep satisfaction.)

HOW THE "YOUS" THAT AREN'T "YOU" KEEP YOU STUCK IN UNHAPPINESS

Because most of our feelings, thoughts, perceptions and actions are a result of our conditioning, the states of consciousness we find ourselves in are also a result of conditioning. And because we are, for the most part, powerless over our conditioning, we are therefore powerless over the high- or low-frequency states of consciousness we find ourselves in and the high and low frequency we attract into our lives.

Imagine yourself to be that tiny, innocent baby born into this world many years ago. You were born with beautiful, unique characteristics all your own. You were born with a blueprint outlining the potentials and possibilities of your life. You were also born open and vulnerable. This was your *essence.* As you grew, you quickly learned how to ensure that your needs for food, shelter and love were met. You did whatever you needed to do (even if it meant denying yourself) in order to gain physical and emotional security. To this end, you may have had to compromise your essential nature — your feelings, needs and special talents. Energy taken from your essence was diverted because the persona which maintained you used this energy to build itself masks to meet the expectations of others.

The extent to which this vital life energy is trapped determines the amount of inner peace, joy, love and fulfillment we can experience. All of us *need* to express our essence. If we do not, we yearn for the happiness we know is our right. But because so much of our energy is held by the false selves of our conditioning, we forget to look within for this happiness. Instead, we look outside to other people, activities and things.

To the extent that we are identified with our conditioning, our awareness of our true feelings, needs and special gifts is blocked. When our energy is held by the false persona, there is little left to use for anything else. The way to return energy trapped by the false self back to our essential nature is to disidentify from false conditioning.

To do this, we must realize that we are more than the sum total of everything we have experienced ourselves to be. We are more than our jobs, feelings, thoughts, beliefs, addictions — even our bodies. Because much of what we think, feel, believe and do has been effected by society, we all have conditioning in common.

Most of us are identified with our bodies to a greater or lesser degree. That is, our state of consciousness is greatly affected by the condition our bodies are in. We are afraid to age for fear of losing health, vitality, attractiveness, prestige, sexuality and personal worth. We believe that a youthful, physically fit body is the source of our greatest power and success. For those of us identified with our bodies in this fashion, the inevitable aging process poses a constant threat to our sense of purpose and well-being. We may spend an enormous amount of effort and money keeping our bodies young and fit so that we may feel good.

We may also be identified with the roles we play in society. We identify with "being something" rather than just "being." Our state of consciousness depends on our success in these roles. (For many of my teenage years I identified with being a dancer. If I lost my balance, "I" failed. I couldn't distinguish between making an error and being flawed as a person. So I quit. Quitting was easier than feeling a failure. Most of us are identified with a role to some degree or another. Think about the roles you play in life.) Are you a wife, mother, father, husband, child, business person, doctor, healer, librarian, teacher, therapist? Identify the roles you play and examine your relationship to them. How dependent is your state of consciousness on their success or failure? What would happen to your state of consciousness if you lost your job or were forced to make a change? Try to assess to what extent you are identified with what you do — that is, to what extent do your roles determine your state of consciousness?

We are also identified with our thoughts, emotions, perceptions and behaviors. When we identify with something, we lose the ability to distinguish between this *partial aspect* of ourselves and the whole self. Feeling angry is the same as being angry. Feeling unworthy is the same as being unworthy. Thinking "I don't deserve" is the same as being undeserving. Behaving compulsively is the same as being compulsive. When we are enmeshed in this way, we have no leverage, no ability to maneuver so that we can change. We become powerless. Identified with anger, we may yell or hit. With grief, we may cry. With fear, we may retreat or fight. *Thinking* we don't deserve, we may overlook opportunities for advancement in our careers. We may sabotage relationships or give up on a project too early. *Believing* there is only one right way to do things may cause us to be judgmental and inflexible.

(Identifying with a thought, feeling or perception renders us powerless over our states of consciousness, which in turn determine how we react to circumstances in our lives. Disidentifying brings mastery over consciousness states and brings power.)

So, let's start learning how to disidentify. I want you to become aware right now that there is a part of you that is able to "stand back" from your feelings so that you may observe them. Get a pen and paper and begin writing. Pretend you are an objective bystander recording everything you perceive about your reactions — your feelings, thoughts and beliefs — to the information presented here so far.

What thoughts have crossed your mind as you've read? What feelings have you had? What beliefs harmonize or conflict with what's been said? Write as objectively and nonjudgmentally as possible. This is an exercise in getting to know the "you" you've been (for the most part) conditioned to be. When you are through, close your eyes. Become aware now of the part of you that has been objective and nonjudgmental. This is the part of you that has been doing the writing. This part of you is your observer. It is not a part of your conditioning.

MEET YOUR OBSERVER

When you are identified with your observer, you are not as identified with your conditioning. The energy that was once diverted and held by the false persona is now partly liberated. The observer holds part of this energy.

As you will see, the observer plays a crucial part in your ability to transform conditioning and manifest divine potential. The observer is open, accepting and nonjudgmental. In a sense, it is the part of you that is void of conditioning, investment and expectation. It is an empty vessel peacefully accepting the ups and downs of life. It is pure breath, energy, awareness. It is aware, without attachment, of what is. It resides peacefully in the "now." It is the unifying center within all that fluctuates and changes in your life.

When you are positioned within the observer, you experience a peaceful state of consciousness. From this vantage point you may observe the variety of conditioning that makes up your false self. As you learn to identify more and more with your observer, you increase your ability to actually navigate yourself out of conditioned ways of being into chosen ways of being. In this sense, the observer becomes not merely a quiet, accepting and detached observer of what is presently activated within you but also the very means by which you take action to gain mastery over your life.

Exercise: Self-Identification[1]

Become aware of your body. For some time, just notice in a neutral way — and without trying to change them — all the physical sensations you can be conscious of. Be aware, for example, of the contact of your body with the chair you are sitting on, of your feet with the ground, of your clothes with your skin. Be aware of your breathing. When you feel you have explored your physical sensations long enough, leave them and go on to the next step.

Become aware of your feelings. What feeling are you experiencing right now? And which are the principal feelings you experience recurrently in your life? Consider both the apparently positive and negative ones: love and irritation, jealousy and tenderness, depression and elation . . . . Do not judge. Just view your usual feelings with the objective attitude of a scientific investigator taking an inventory. When you are satisfied, shift your attention from this area and proceed to the next step.

Turn your attention to your desires. Adopting the same impartial attitude as before, review the main desires which take turns in motivating your life. Often you may well be identified with one or the other of these but now you simply consider them, side by side. Finally, leave your desires and continue with the next step.

Observe the world of your thoughts. As soon as a thought emerges, watch it until another one takes its place, then another one, and so on. If you think you are not having any thoughts, realize that this too is a thought. Watch your stream of consciousness as it flows by: memories, opinions, nonsense, arguments, images. Do this for a couple

---

[1]This exercise is from Piero Ferrucci, *What We May Be* (Los Angeles: J.P. Tarcher, 1982), pp. 66-67.

of minutes, then dismiss this realm as well from your observation.

The observer — the one who has been watching your sensations, feelings, desires, and thoughts — is not the same as the object it observes. *Who* is it that has been observing all these realms? It is your *self.* The self is not an image or a thought; it is that essence which has been observing all these realms and yet is distinct from all of them. And you are that being. Say inwardly: "I am the *self,* a center of pure consciousness." Seek to realize this for about two minutes.

Exercise: Think of Disidentifying

When you find yourself embroiled in a particular state of consciousness, think of disidentifying. I like to use the phrase "I take my identity out of _____." Thus, if I find myself overwhelmed with anxiety or fear, I may say, "I take my identity out of fear and surrender to higher power." Thinking this way helps bring my awareness around to the fact that I am enmeshed in my conditioning. I may then choose to work with fear in any of the number of ways described later in this book.

Exercise: Self-Observation

The goal here is to become aware of the many ways you are identified with your conditioning and to become more and more identified with your observer. For one to two weeks keep a journal of observations about yourself. You may want to pick a time in the evening in which to review your day. Notice how you have related to (1) your body; (2) your job; (3) your friends, spouse and children; and (4) other miscellaneous circumstances and events.

Observe your feelings, thoughts and behaviors in a nonjudgmental manner. Write these observations down. The skill you acquire and the information that you accumulate will be useful later when you begin using light-fire to transform your life.

NAVIGATING

Navigating is the ability to direct the movement of awareness.

John comes home late from work. He's had a hard day, and all he wants is to eat a warm dinner, take a long soak in the tub and go to sleep.

Instead, Sally, his wife, greets him with glaring eyes. "Where have you been?" she yells. "Dinner has been ready for over an hour. No one answered at the office when I called. Why didn't you call me?" Everything in him wants to pick up the lamp and hit her over the head! He feels helpless. He is pissed. He reacts to these onslaughts unconsciously and uncontrollably. Punching his fist into the door, he turns around and walks out.

John and Sally are both victims of their conditioning and their state of consciousness. The whole of their *awareness* is *trapped* within the state of consciousness in which they find themselves. In order for John and Sally to gain mastery over their lives, they will have to learn how to *navigate* with at least a portion of their awareness into another state of consciousness. If they had been able to do this, they would have been able to move *away* from their respective angry responses and into the accepting center of the observer. Both would have then been able to follow through with any number of possible alternative responses to the situation.

Because John was incapable of this, he was victimized by his own conditioned response, and he paid the price — hurting his hand, aggravating his relationship with Sally, losing the rest and relaxation he desired so much. So did Sally pay a price — eating dinner alone, suffering indigestion, perhaps eventually losing her relationship with John.

The ability to navigate through consciousness is essential in gaining mastery over your life. You must become objective to your states of consciousness and be able to direct your awareness away from or into those states at will. You may move with awareness into your physical body, your perceptions, your emotions and your thoughts. A good way to begin is to practice directing your awareness within and throughout the many facets of your physical body.

Exercise: Navigating Through the Spaces of Your Body

Begin by focusing your awareness or attention in the center of your head — your midbrain — the point that is midway between your ears and halfway between your eyes and the back of your head. Now slowly move your attention away from that spot upward to the crown of your head, then downward into your feet, and then fluidly within the spaces of your body (chest, arms, neck, stomach, hips, legs, ankles, feet.) Do this slowly, and see if you can get a sense of how each part of your body is feeling as you go.

If you find this difficult to do, start again by focusing in your midbrain. Then imagine a little person inside that spot, and watch as he or she takes an exploratory journey within the spaces of your body. As this little person travels throughout your body, stay in communication with him or her. Ask the little person specifically how he or she feels being in each of these respective areas. At this time there is no need to do anything about what the little person or you feels. Just observe.

The preceding exercise will strengthen your ability to navigate. When you can do this exercise easily, go on to the next one.

Exercise: Navigating Through Feelings and Sensations

Close your eyes.   Become aware of a predominant feeling or sensation.   Try to locate where you experience this feeling in your body. For example, many of us feel fear as a tightening in the chest, throat or stomach. Now move with your awareness (or little person) into the center of the feeling in your body.   With your awareness, again explore the total area of this sensation.   Ask yourself or your person, "How does it feel to be here?"   "What does the feeling/sensation communicate or express?"

Now move away from the feeling sensation into an area of your body that feels open and free. How does it feel to be here? Allow yourself (or little person) to move from one area to the other. Note the felt difference between the two. Know that both states of consciousness exist at once within the body-mind you call "you."

Fundamental to the success of this exercise is the understanding that *more than one consciousness state is operating within you at one time*. Which of the two consciousness states (fear or openness, in the example) do you tend to identify with more? Your key to mastery is your ability to maneuver your awareness away from the consciousness you find yourself in and into the consciousness of your choice. Thus, if you tend to focus more on fear, move with awareness away from fear and into openness. If you tend to deny fear and focus on openness, move into the fear and start exploring this aspect of yourself.

The ability to navigate also enables you to move away from a conditioned state of consciousness and into your observing center. (You will know you have navigated into your observing center when you feel a shift in awareness. This shift occurs as you move away from a feeling of being "taken over" or "overwhelmed" by a state of consciousness into an experience of subtle detachment. I say subtle because the shift can be ever so minor. You feel the consciousness state just as strongly, but a tiny part of you is standing back looking in. The shift may be accompanied by a sigh of relief, as a knowing that "I can handle this" seeps into awareness. You feel the emotion, but now there is a willingness to work with it and learn from it. Relief comes as you realize, "I am now in control; the emotion is not." This is very different from feeling lost within an emotion, from feeling "the emotion has control over me."

It is possible to transform any state of consciousness but not without the ability to move into it or away from it at will. Navigating with awareness into fear (for example) enables you to go beyond the appearance of it and maneuver into the center or originating cause of it. Navigating away from fear allows you to (1) identify with your observer, (2) identify with a different or more empowering state of consciousness, or (3) identify with a higher aspect of yourself.

UPPER ROOM
YOUR GATEWAY TO HIGHER CONSCIOUSNESS

It is well known that what some of the ancient metaphysical practices called chakras are indeed physical energy centers or vortexes interpenetrating the physical body. There are apparently seven to nineteen of these centers (depending on whose model you are following), that can be felt and/or seen by sensitive individuals open to perceiving them. Each one of these centers corresponds to a particular aspect of human consciousness. (For more information about the chakras, see Suggested Reading, pp. 153-156.)

One of these centers, known as the upper room, is located six to twelve inches above the top of the head and is the center of higher consciousness. For thousands of years, the art of navigating into this center as a step to achieving enlightenment was practiced only by a privileged few. Learning to move with awareness into this center of higher consciousness helps to open you to the radiant awareness of your higher self. The higher self is always present within and throughout every aspect of the personality system. It is only your conditioning that prevents you from being aware of this presence in the minute-to-minute activity of your life. Rising above the head allows you to move up and out of the conditioning of your personality system, which blocks this awareness. In so doing, you move right into the center of higher consciousness.

Exercise: Moving into Your Upper Room[1]

Close your eyes. Move with your awareness to your midbrain. Imagine a line rising vertically up and out of your head. Move with your awareness along this imaginary line until you "feel" your awareness coming to rest in the center of an energy vortex (six to twelve inches above the top of your head). This is your upper room. Let your brain relax. With your awareness, explore this room. See if you can move right into its center, immersing yourself in the power, peace and radiance that lie within it.

Exercise: Practicing Dual-Focused Awareness

As you continue to read try to remain focused in your upper room. You can do this by softening your eyes — that is, rather than "looking outwardly" at the words on the page, you "allow" the words to come into your field of vision. As you read, most of your attention is focused inwardly and upwardly, within your upper room. Only a small part of your attention is "allowing" the words to enter your awareness.

Learning to divide your awareness like this — between something that is happening outside of you and something that is happening inside of you — will bring greater mastery over your consciousness states. With practice, you will eventually be able to go about all the activities of your life, while remaining focused in this center of higher consciousness. When you do this, you will be amazed at the profound effect this will have on

---

[1]This exercise is used with permission from the school of Actualism, headquartered in Costa Mesa, California.

your state of consciousness and therefore on the circumstances of your life.

Staying focused in your upper room for long periods of time is a form of meditation. It brings with it enlightened and expanded states of consciousness. With attention focused here, you become an open channel for the higher energies of the universe — your personality becomes a vehicle through which to manifest the higher self that you actually are.

The danger of staying focused in the upper room may be apparent to you. From this place in consciousness it is all too easy to "space out" — that is, lose your sense of reality or have difficulty functioning.

It is not the goal of this book to teach merely the attainment of higher consciousness. Rather, the goal is to show how to bring higher consciousness "down" or "out" into daily life. Most of us do not have the luxury of sitting on a mountaintop seeking enlightenment. We have jobs to do, children to raise, responsibilities to keep, the stewardship of a planet to maintain. The goal here is to describe a way of awakening to higher consciousness while maintaining the daily activities of our lives.

Exercise: Directing Radiant Consciousness into Your Body and Field[2]

Navigate with your awareness once again into your upper room. Take a minute to experience the power, peace and radiance that are present within.

Allow your brain to relax and think of this radiant consciousness flowing down from your upper room into the spaces of your brain. You may experience this as a form of connecting, as the spaces of your brain merge with the spaces of your upper room. It is as if the two let down their barriers and become one. Because the brain is the center of mental activity, you will be enlightening your *knowing* awareness.

---

[2]School of Actualism, used with permission.

Now think of radiant consciousness flowing into the neurons of your brain and all the neural pathways of your body. Let go of the thought, and allow yourself to experience the radiant consciousness moving throughout your nervous system. There is an instantaneous grounding effect. Your awareness is no longer floating on top of your head but is instead focused throughout the totality of your body. This may at first feel as if you are losing your "high," but you are not. It is only becoming more dispersed. Doing this will enlighten your *sensory* awareness because the nervous system is the center of this activity.

Now think of radiant consciousness flowing from your upper room into your heart, blood, liver and glands. These form the core of your emotional nature. Let the radiant consciousness move through and enlighten your *feeling* awareness.

As you practice this meditation daily you will find that your mental, emotional and perceptual natures will increasingly reflect the higher consciousness of this upper room. I cannot overemphasize how important this is. The conditioning factors affecting the mental, emotional and perceptual natures of your personality system drag you down into lower states of consciousness. Enlightening them by directing radiant consciousness into and throughout these systems will help free them of conditioned programming. This in turn will free you of conditioned programming and enable you to think, feel and perceive the way of your divine essence.

TRANSFORMING CONDITIONING

Even though learning to navigate away from conditioning into the higher consciousness of the upper room is valuable, it is not enough. Navigating will help you rise above conditioning, but it won't help you transform it. Transformation is what happens when the personality actually releases its conditioning and aligns its way of thinking, feeling, perceiving and behaving with that of its divine nature. In order to do this, the energy that has been trapped by the false conditioned persona must be released and returned to essence (our true feelings, needs and special talents).

We all know people who although very spiritual can't seem to get their acts together. They meditate everyday, go to church regularly, faithfully read the *Bible* or throw the *I Ching*, but their lives never seem to improve. They seem adept at "rising above" their conditioning, but they are not very good at manifesting the divine in their lives.

When I was twenty-four years old, I experienced a higher power temporarily manifest itself in my life. I lived in an expanded state of awareness for a few weeks, but that did not help the fact that I was lonely, poor and terribly powerless over my addictions. I was an example of someone being in a highly spiritual state yet still trapped by false conditioned programming. A good way to describe how I felt at that time would be to say I was ecstatic and miserable all at once. My highest consciousness could not change the miserable conditions of my life.

If our conditioning affects our thinking, feeling, perceiving and behaving, it follows that we will have to learn how to transform these ways of being. If we want to change our lives for the better — if we want to live with greater joy, love, creativity and abundance in our day-to-day existence — in order to awaken to this potential we will have to transform the very substance of our conditioning. This transformation must occur in such a way as to *mirror or reflect the higher consciousness and actual design of our essence.*

The way to effect this kind of change is to transform a low-frequency state of consciousness into a high-frequency state of consciousness. As a reminder, whenever I speak of low-frequency states of consciousness, I am speaking of "negative" states of consciousness that collect in our physical, perceptual, emotional and mental systems. These states are what we call hate, rage, anger, fear, guilt, grief, ill-will, confusion, idealization, rigidity and judgmentalism. Low-frequency states drag us down; they tend to drag others down as well. They are the mental-emotional-perceptual equivalents of toxic wastes in our physical environment. They contaminate and pollute our minds, our feelings and those of others.

One powerful way of transforming these states is to direct light-energy into our bodies and energy fields.[1] These aspects of ourselves hold consciousness within their structures. Because emotional pain (from mild to acute) result from an aggregate of low-frequency consciousness states, one crucial technique for moving through pain is the channeling and directing of light-

---

[1]Scientific investigation has told us that everything in the universe is energy and that energy exists in two forms: radiation and matter. Human beings, like all living organisms, are in fact complex energy structures in which energy is both radiating and bound as matter. Beyond the energy making up the physical body, ancient and contemporary explorers have determined that the human body exists in an energy field that radiates beyond the body mass. For more information about this, see Suggested Reading, pp.153-156.

energy. I have found that whenever I have chosen to meditate using my source of light and channeling that energy into the spaces of my body, I have been able to uplift and enlighten my states of consciousness.

Each low-frequency state has a corresponding high-frequency state. Emotionally, if I feel hate, it is likely I will experience more love after the light penetration. Mentally, if I am confused, it is likely I will experience greater clarity. Perceptually, if I feel stuck and rigid, it is likely I will become more open and flexible. The high-frequency states of wisdom, love and creativity affect every aspect of our lives. In order to be fulfilled, it is essential that these three qualities express themselves throughout the personality. When blocked due to conditioning, each one has a corresponding low-frequency state. In order to change our lives to reflect the higher consciousness of our divine nature, it is up to us to release the high-frequency consciousness trapped within low-frequency states.

The energy band of wisdom at its lower frequency level produces what we experience as fear. Fear comes from a sense of unknowing. What we don't know we fear. Fear is a form of protection. It produces caution. Fear alerts us to potential danger. So does wisdom. The difference between fear and wisdom, however, is that fear is blind and usually results in a fight or flight response, even when inappropriate, whereas wisdom arms us with a peaceful sense of knowing. Wisdom results in decisive right action based on a clear assessment of the problem. Fear causes us to act blindly, hurriedly and indecisively — often leading us astray. When we lose a job, fear alerts us to the potential danger of our decreased ability to sustain survival. If we are motived by fear, however, we may not do what's best for our overall well-being. We may take the first job that comes along, overriding our spiritual needs for challenge and stimulation. If, however, we transmute fear to wisdom, we will be able to clearly assess and weigh the needs of the total self. This will enable us to ascertain how long our financial resources will last so that we may calmly look for what we truly desire in a job.

Knowing that fear is the low-frequency version of wisdom, we can choose to lift the consciousness of the fear so that we may open to the higher wisdom present within. A new client came to see me one afternoon. As we talked, it became clear that she lacked self-confidence. Although she had many excellent and creative ideas, she was paralyzed by fear. I had her close her eyes. As we began channeling light-energy, a black form came to her and told her he was her fear. He went on to explain to her that he was there to give her strength. But she didn't want his strength because she didn't want to gain strength from fear. Understandably so. I had her surround him in a clear, crystal light. Almost immediately this frightening figure shed his black shroud and became a radiant man. He told her he was there to let her know she was a beautiful, talented and gifted person and that he'd always be there for her to remind her of that fact when she was overwhelmed or paralyzed by fear. She left my office filled with an enormous sense of safety and well-being — a very different state of consciousness than the one she had arrived in. Fear carries wisdom within it. This wise part of her covered in the black shroud of fear had all the wisdom she needed to heal at that moment.

Fear can be felt as a mental cloud that inhibits clear vision. Without this clarity, we act randomly and/or look to others for answers. We hold onto rules and "shoulds," giving ourselves a false sense of security; then we fall hard when past rules no longer sustain changing situations.

Everything changes, and if we want to flow effortlessly with the change we must learn how to let go of these rules. In their place we need a substantial yet fluid foundation that moves with our evolving needs and guides us with a sense of knowing. This is wisdom at its best. In touch with wisdom, we minimize any doubt or confusion. We act clearly and decisively according to higher direction.

When vibrating at its lower frequency, the energy band of love, which covers a much broader range of qualities than we typically associate with the word, produces hate or rage at worst and indifference at best. Without high-frequency love we may feel estranged, at odds with the rest of humanity. We may wonder if there is something deeply wrong with us. We cannot love others because it is impossible to give what we do not have. We cannot love life because life is dull. We have lost our ability to simply enjoy the sensory pleasures of living — the smells, feels, tastes, sights and sounds of our incredibly lush environment.[2]

It is difficult to change a consciousness state of hate into one of love by simply thinking about love. Some of my clients have said to me privately, "I know I should be loving myself, but saying 'I love you' to the mirror feels stupid and just doesn't seem to change the way I really feel about myself inside." Positive affirmations are powerful and useful tools, but they are only part of the picture. I use them in conjunction with light-fire. When I recognize the low-frequency inversion of love, I send energy into every cell, molecule and atom of my body. As I am released of hate and filled with love, I then use the added power of thought to program or anchor this newfound energy into my psyche and to bring into

---

[2]We have lost this ability, in part, as an emotional protection against the usurpation of our natural environment by a one-dimensional, techno-plastic environment. The experience of a "void" by so many individuals may in fact be a natural outcome of our modern age — one in which we have for the most part been severed from our natural environment — its beauty and power. In my mind the personal void is as much a social and political issue as it is a psychological and spiritual one. This book, however, attempts to address this problem from the perspective of the latter only. It is my hope that by restoring a sense of value, purpose, joy and creativity in enough individuals, the collective creative power will be found to rectify our global condition.

awareness deeper layers of hatred which I can then process with light-fire.[3]

Like fish in the sea, we are so immersed in our culture's repression of true creativity, few of us even recognize this repression as an issue. Ironically for a society that prides itself on its ingenuity and innovation, our educational system and widespread dysfunctionality stifle the development of our most profound creative expressions. Much of the malaise, boredom and apathy we see all around us stems from individuals being cut off from their inner creative sources. People obsessed with relationships, work, drugs, food or any other addictive substance or process have a hole within themselves that they can conceive of filling only in that manner. That hole is the vacuum that occurs when our creative energies are not allowed to flow, to excite, to bring visions, to inspire action and to create ever-renewing realities.

The high-frequency creative energies can be fragile. Typical parenting and educational practices usually cut them off at their inner source. Public recognition of creativity is restricted to its formal expression in the "arts," a segregated section of society in which only a few extraordinary individuals can make a living, or in a field such as advertising, which often carries the connotation of "creative prostitution."

Most of us are intimately aware of the lack of high-frequency creative energy in our lives; we feel a gnawing sense that this is not the way life should be, that something is missing. True creativity is a state of being and may exist in any and all areas of our lives. With it,

---

[3]Have you noticed that when you say a positive affirmation, the opposite feeling often comes into your awareness? Saying "I deserve wealth" or "I am beautiful" often activates feelings of unworthiness — all those doubts and fears that lie below awareness. Saying "I am beautiful" again and again will not make you feel beautiful if you do not. If you use the affirmation, however, to bring low frequency into your awareness, you may then use the light tools to transform and release these lower states of consciousness (see Parts 3 and 4). When combined with tools that have the power to actually transmute energy, positive affirmation can be a powerful tool for change.

we can mold the form our lives take, just as a sculptor molds with plaster or clay. With it, we may build beautiful inner and outer environments; we may attune our inner ears to the music of the heavens; we may move our bodies in rhythm to the natural flow of life's seasons; we may extend beyond our limitations, transcending all that we've ever been and more. True creativity fills our lives with meaning. When we are in touch with this basic power, the world becomes an exciting place filled with infinite possibility and hope. Inspiration guides our action.

The experience of any lack or void in our lives is our felt absence of these three energies. Without wisdom, we act randomly, wandering aimlessly about with no inner sense of appropriate action. Without love, we lack the inner support to risk being ourselves in the world. Without creativity, we lack energy, spontaneity, inspiration and hope. To fill this discontent we must open (1) to the higher wisdom that floods our life with meaning; (2) to love for self, others and humanity; and (3) to our creative inspirations.

Wisdom, love and creativity are basic. They are part of our essence. We do not have to learn how to channel them. We know this already. We need only to learn how to raise our consciousness so that we may unlock the potential that lies within.

78

TRANSFORMING
WITH LIGHT

Light comes from our source. People with extended or extrasensory perception can see our light bodies. Kirlian photography can photograph it. Even I, who am not normally open in this way, have seen the light that interpenetrates the denser physical body.

The process of directing light into the mass of the body is one I have practiced regularly for more than fifteen years. Most mornings I have meditated on inner light penetrating every organ, cell, molecule and atom of my body, and I have discovered that whenever I choose, I can uplift whatever low-frequency state I am in with this process.

Light Reveals

In much the same way as a candle illuminates an attic, inner light reveals the cobwebs and debris of our low-frequency programming. They are all there within us. We just don't see them, at least not until we do the same old thing again and again with unrewarding results. Then, maybe, we sit up and take notice. We say, "Gee, maybe I'm doing something wrong here!"

Now let's imagine that you can take a trip into this attic of your body-mind. Here all about you, but hidden from sight, are the cobwebs of your conditioning. You do not need them and you do not want them anymore, but they hang around because you can't see them. You want them out because they are making your life miserable, but you can't get to them because it's just too dark to see.

Then someone hands you a candle. You see a hazy form right under your nose. You bring the candlelight closer, becoming aware of the complex interweavings of the form of this conditioned web. Now you understand it. You see it. You know where it is. "Finally," you think, "I can do something about it!"

This is how inner light works. You shine light into the nooks and crannies of unconsciousness and become conscious. You may shine light into your physical body and field, and you may shine it into your mental, emotional and perceptual natures. When you focus light within, whatever is not in high-frequency states of consciousness will be revealed.

This works in much the same way as taking white chalk and coloring on black paper — both stand out in contrast. When you channel light into a low-frequency state such as anger, the anger becomes more apparent by contrast. When you channel light into love, the two blend together beautifully. If you are angry and know you are angry, you do not need to use inner light in this way. But if you have a load of anger simmering below the surface — leaking out in all sorts of manipulative ways — using light will help bring this anger into your awareness.

Sometimes when you channel light, you become aware of obstructions. These may appear as patches of darkness and may feel uncomfortable. Discomfort is a form of low-frequency consciousness, and it passes as the low frequency is processed. (I use the word "process" to mean the transmutation of low-frequency consciousness into high-frequency consciousness.)

When doing the exercise that follows (Downpour with Light), you may notice that the light flows easily and fluidly through certain parts of your body but not through others. This is common. Your body has consciousness. It may feel good at times; at other times, it may not. Parts of your body may feel better than other parts. Until you start channeling light, you are largely unconscious of this variation. Then you may notice that your stomach feels like lead, or your neck is tight and constricted, or the light "just won't go into your hips." Light reveals the low-frequency states of consciousness which block awakening to your higher nature.

Light is a form of energy, and like all forms of energy, it abides by certain laws. One such law — **thought directs energy** — and its counterpart — **energy follows thought** — are the foundation on which this work is based. The work of channeling energy is directed by the power of thought.

You begin by thinking of the light; then you let go of the thought so that you may experience what is happening. Holding onto a thought keeps the energy in the head. To let the energy flow, you must relax the brain and let go of the thought.

Here is a an exercise to get you started. Remember: think the thought, let go of the thought and let yourself experience what happens as light begins to penetrate the physical spaces of your body and field. As you do this, observe without judgment what you experience. There is no right or wrong. Be aware of the light. Be aware of the darkness. Be aware of whatever sensations, thoughts or feelings are activated within you. Whatever you experience is coming into your awareness because you are ready to deal with it.

Exercise: Downpour with Light[1]

Sit comfortably in a chair, feet flat on the floor, hands on your thighs, palms facing downward. Close your eyes and let your mind relax.

Move with your awareness into your upper room. Think of a point of light here expanding in size to approximately three inches in diameter and

---

[1] School of Actualism, used with permission.

becoming a luminous, crystalline white star-sun. Think of this sun opening and showering a great flood of energy. Experience this energy downpouring through your body and out the bottoms of your feet, cleansing and washing away all toxic debris, leaving you feeling fresh and clean.

Slowly and one area at a time, think of intensifying the light-energy in your head, neck, shoulders, arms, hands, chest, stomach, pelvic area, legs and feet.

Think of your feet closing and experience as this downpour of crystalline white light-energy starts to back up from below and fill every cell and pore of your body. Notice as it pours out of an opening in the top of your head into the field that surrounds your body. Let your body-field soak up this wonderful, pure white light-energy.

Sit still with this for awhile and let yourself feel the purified energy pouring into every part of you — body, mind, emotions. Slowly open your eyes and observe the changes that are happening within.

Light-Fire Transforms

Let's return to the attic for a moment. You are now face to face with a huge web of conditioning. You can see it clear as day. Perhaps its form manifests as a dark spot in your body or field, or perhaps you register it as some form of low-frequency consciousness such as sadness, rage or worry. You are now in the position to effect permanent change by transforming this particular web.

Two other laws of energy state that **where obstruction to life-energy exists, there is discomfort (from mild to acute pain)** and that **where thought is held, the power of life energy is focused.** When you become aware of discomfort, you may use your power of thought to direct the light-energy right into the center of the block. Sometimes this is all you have to do to free the trapped energy.

There are times, however, when low-frequency conditioning is just too strong and pervasive. At these times, you can use the fire aspect of light to actually burn away low-frequency conditioning. It is the use of light-fire that has the greatest potential to effect change. Fire literally burns away or consumes the obstruction to life energy flow. Light-fire transmutes low-frequency consciousness into high-frequency consciousness. When this happens, you burn away only what is false to your true nature and release the energy trapped or held within the low frequency back to your essence.

Light-fire cannot burn away essence. So if you are not sure if a particular aspect of yourself is essence or conditioning, a good way to find out is by focusing the fire on it. If it is false conditioning, it will go. If it is essence, it will get stronger.

Never be afraid of working in this way. Fire only burns away what you are ready to release. Why? Because the light only works on your behalf. All of your conditioned blocks to life energy flow are there to teach you lessons. If you have not yet learned them, no amount of light will take this opportunity from you. Light helps you learn faster by revealing what you need to work on and by burning away the baggage you no longer need to carry around.

Working with fire is no different than working with light. Think of your light sun becoming a burning flame, and then let go of the thought and experience what happens.

Exercise: Working with Light-Fire[2]

Do the Downpour with Light (p. 81). After you feel your body and field filled with light, focus your awareness on obstructions to life energy flow. These may manifest as dark spaces within your

---

[2]School of Actualism, used with permission.

body and field or as low-frequency feelings (anger, sadness), thoughts (obsession, confusion) or beliefs ("I'm no good," "I don't deserve it").

Think (and let go) of the light filling and surrounding the low frequency. Now think of your sun becoming an inner ball of fire that intensifies within the area of the blockage. Allow some time for the burning process to complete itself. When you feel an inner shift or a lift, the work has been completed.

Then think of the fire coming to a halt. Be aware of the spaces within that have been emptied of low-frequency consciousness by the fire. Immediately think of light pouring back into those spaces, filling them with high-frequency energy. Stay with this assimilation period for a while (at least ten minutes). Allow yourself to open and experience as light-energy fills every organ and cell of your body-field and every aspect of your body-mind consciousness. (If you do not take the time to assimilate the light-energy back into the empty spaces, you leave them open to be refilled with more low-frequency energy.)

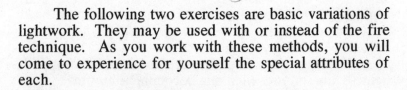

The following two exercises are basic variations of lightwork. They may be used with or instead of the fire technique. As you work with these methods, you will come to experience for yourself the special attributes of each.

Exercise: Spinning[3]

Begin by doing Downpour with Light.

Refocus in your upper room. Become aware of the three-inch sun. Think of that sun expanding in size to approximately three and a half feet in diameter. As it expands it rises to a place about three feet above the top of your head. Now think of

---

[3]School of Actualism, used with permission.

this sun arcing down in front of your body and coming to a rest at a point three feet below the bottom of your feet. Think of the sun spinning in the direction opposite from that of the hands of a clock (from the perspective of looking down). This creates a powerful vacuum action. As the sun begins to travel up your body, it vacuums out physical, perceptual, emotional and mental low-frequency debris.

Think of the sun slowly traveling upwardly, first enveloping your feet and lower legs. Let it continue to spin here for a few minutes; then allow the sun to continue on up until your pelvic area is enclosed within the spinning sun. Rest a couple of minutes. Let the sun continue on up to envelop your upper torso. Rest. Up to your head and shoulders. Rest. Up above the top of your head. Continue here for a couple of minutes before asking the sun to come to a halt.

Now arc the sun down again to the bottom of your field. This time think of it spinning in the direction of the hands of a clock (clockwise). The sun begins to deposit light-energy back into the spaces that have been emptied of debris. The sun slowly moves upwardly through your body as it did before and comes to rest above the top of your head. (IMPORTANT: Always be sure to end this exercise with the *clockwise* spinning. Failing to do so will leave the spaces of your body open to low-frequency energy. If you have a tendency to fall asleep in the middle of meditations don't do this exercise right before you go to bed.)

Spend at least ten minutes assimilating this powerful technique. Think of high-frequency light-energy flowing into every organ and cell of your body-field and every aspect of your body-mind consciousness.

Exercise: Magnetic/Dynamic Action of Sun[4]

Begin by doing Downpour with Light.

Expand your sun to the size of your energy field[5] or to whatever size feels naturally comfortable. Think of the sun becoming a large magnet that powerfully draws into itself low-frequency states of consciousness that are ready to go. Stay with this until you feel a release.

Think of the fire consuming the low-frequency consciousness. Ask the sun to dynamically send high-frequency light-energy back into your spaces. Let the spaces of your body and field open fully to receive this healing energy. Assimilate this for at least ten minutes.

You may also want to experiment with decreasing or increasing the size of the sun. Doing this will focus and intensify the energy in specific areas of your body. For example, if you feel constricted in your heart area, shrinking the sun down in size and aligning the center of the sun with the heart area will specifically focus its magnetic/dynamic action. You may also expand the sun to surround your room or house. In this way, you will clear low-frequency consciousness that tends to collect in and pollute the environment.

---

[4]School of Actualism, used with permission.

[5]This will vary from individual to individual. If you have never done lightwork or any other form of energy work, your energy field probably extends a short distance out from your body. The more work you've done enlightening your field, the larger it can be.

TWO-WAY FLOW OF LOVE AND GRATITUDE

Whenever I sit down to work with radiant consciousness and/or light, I always begin by thanking and blessing the higher self that I am. Blessing and giving thanks are age-old customs. Unfortunately, they have lost their meaning and power in our hurried and superficial society. Whenever we thank the universe for what we have, we are sending it positive energy. This positive energy attracts more positive energy and so our riches multiply.

When we thank and bless our higher source, we are acknowledging its very important place in our lives. This is a powerful message to the personality that life is divine, not merely conditioned. These messages are powerful reprogramming tools. Whenever we bless the divine in our lives, we attract more of the divine to us. Whenever you are upset by something, bless it. Whenever you are upset by somebody, bless him or her. Bless yourself. What you hate most about yourself, bless it. Bless your fat. Bless your stupidity. Bless your addiction. Bless your pride. Bless your stubbornness. If you don't like it, bless it.[1]

[1]An excellent tape for this is Louise Hay, *Morning and Evening Meditation* (Santa Monica, CA: Hay House, 1983). Available through the LivingQuest catalog. (See Resources, pp. 151-152.)

Exercise: Love and Gratitude[2]

Move with your awareness into your upper room. Feel the peace, power, radiance and love emanating from this seat of higher consciousness.

Meditate on your higher self or higher power. Just think of it to amplify its felt presence in your life.

When you feel it, send a thought of love and gratitude. Thank it for everything it has given you. (Do not focus on what you don't have. You do that only when you are in light-fire, processing conditioned programming.) If you can't seem to find anything to be grateful for, try this for starts: your eyesight; your legs that carry you from place to place; your hands with which you eat, carry, write; the food on your table; the roof over your head; your soft bed to sleep on; any loved one in your life — you get the idea!

Open to receive the love and gratitude pouring from your higher self into you, its creation. Know that you are invaluable to it and are loved unconditionally. Without you, the personality, your higher self would have no vehicle through which to express.

Focus on and amplify this two-way flow of love and gratitude between you and your higher self.

---

[2]School of Actualism, used with permission.

CREATING A HEALING SPACE

Much of the transformation process entails becoming aware of pain (emotional or physical) and then moving into the center of the pain to discover its source. This process may feel *as if* the situation is getting worse. Because of the nature of this kind of work, it is good to provide for ourselves comfortable and safe outer and inner environments. I always begin with an inner light meditation so that I feel connected with my higher self before working with low-frequency consciousness. This enables me to stay centered in the light of the divine while I am processing fear, anger, judgment, and so on.

The following visualization will help you to create a safe inner space. I would suggest that for best results, each time you sit down to do an exercise from Parts 3 and 4 of this book, you first do the Daily Meditation (pp. 91-92) and create a healing space. This will provide you with the optimum inner environment for transformational work.

Exercise: Creating Your Healing Space

Begin with the Daily Meditation.

Refocus your awareness in your upper room. Spend at least five minutes experiencing the higher consciousness of this energy center. Think of your higher self and magnify your relationship to it.

Think of your upper room expanding in size. Notice yourself now seated comfortably within this magnificent room. Become aware of your observer and higher self seated here with you. Spend some time looking around, becoming familiar with the smells, textures, sights and sounds. Think of a soft light within the center of the room radiating outwardly until its rays touch the lighted boundaries. If you wish, you may increase the density of the light on the periphery to create a light shield for greater protection. (For more information, see pp. 137-138.) Take as much time as you need to make this space comfortable and safe for your healing work.

DAILY MEDITATION
Suggested time: 15 - 40 minutes

The following is a combination of four previous exercises.[1] When combined, they make up a simple yet thorough light session that may be used each morning or evening for simple regeneration or as the basis of further in-depth processing. Please do this meditation at least once before experimenting with the exercises in Parts 3 and 4.

Sit comfortably in a chair, feet flat on the floor, hands on your thighs, palms facing downward. Close your eyes and let your mind relax.

Moving into Your Upper Room: Close your eyes. Navigate with your awareness to your midbrain. From here travel along an imaginary line until you "feel" your awareness coming to rest in the center of an energy vortex (six to twelve inches above the top of your head) — your upper room. Let your brain relax. With your awareness, explore this room. See if you can move right into its center, immersing yourself in the power, peace and radiance that lie within it.

Two-Way Flow of Love and Gratitude: Become aware of your higher self. Just think of it to amplify its felt presence in your life. When you can feel its presence, send a thought of love and gratitude. Thank it for everything it has given you. Experience the love and gratitude your higher self has for you. Magnify this two-way flow of love and gratitude.

Directing Radiant Consciousness: (Remember: think the thought, let go of the thought and experience what happens.) Allow your brain to relax and think of the radiant consciousness of your upper room flowing down into the spaces of your brain and enlightening your knowing awareness.

---

[1] School of Actualism, used with permission.

Now think of radiant consciousness flowing into the neurons of your brain and all the neural pathways of your body. Allow yourself to experience what it feels like to have radiant consciousness moving throughout your nervous system and enlightening sensory awareness.

Now think of radiant consciousness flowing from your upper room into your heart, blood, liver and glands and enlightening feeling awareness.

Experience as all three — knowing, sensory, and feeling awareness — are simultaneously gathered, uplifted and enlightened.

Downpour with Light: Move with your awareness into your upper room. Think of a point of light floating, expanding in size to approximately three inches in diameter, becoming a luminous, crystalline white star-sun. Think of this sun opening and showering a great flood of energy. Experience this energy downpouring through your body and out the bottoms of your feet, cleansing and washing away all toxic debris, leaving you feeling fresh and clean.

Slowly and one area at a time, think of intensifying the light-energy in your head, neck, shoulders, arms, hands, chest, stomach, pelvic area, legs and feet.

Think of your feet closing, and experience as this downpour of crystalline white light-energy starts to back up from below and fill every cell and pore of your body. Notice as it pours out of an opening in the top of your head into the field that surrounds your body. Let your body-field soak up this wonderful, pure white light-energy.

Sit still with this for awhile, and let yourself feel the purified energy pouring into every part of you. Slowly open your eyes and observe the changes that are happening within.

Send love to your higher self. Open to receive love and gratitude back. Magnify this two-way flow.

Optional: Create your healing space for additional work.

PART THREE

TRANSFORMATION OF IDENTITY

The shrieking of my two boys outside the door wakes me with a start. "Should I go out?" I wonder. "No. Gene's out there. He can take care of this crisis. No different from any other morning." I roll over toward the wall and stare into space. The sounds of children subside, moving out of focus. My mind shifts gear as "Mother" in me recedes and "Author" takes over. "The book's not working. Something's still missing. Perhaps it needs more personal examples throughout the main body of text." I look at the clock. 9:00 A.M. Late. But I didn't get to bed until 3:00 A.M. "Just can't seem to make it all work." I'm on my back now, staring at the ceiling, my eyes wide open. I can still feel the caffeine I had last night rumbling through my nervous system. "That 'decaffeinated' Earl Gray did have some caffeine," my "Health Manager" says disgruntledly.

Author: "Well, I'll have to have more to keep me going. Can't afford to be tired today."

Health Manager: "Okay, but just this morning. I've got to have time to detox before this evening so I can get some sleep."

I'm out of bed, on the floor doing a shoulder stand for my back. I stand up, do a few bends from the waist, grab some clean sheets of paper and take a seat in my favorite chair. Closing my eyes, I breathe deeply and prepare to journey inwardly into light. Within the center of me I feel the voices of "Mother," "Author" and "Health Manager" slowly become silent. Only stillness now as I travel into higher dimensions of my inner world. I connect with my creative energy source and anchor it well into my body, preparing to function from my "Author" identity most of the day. Ideas begin to flow and I begin to write.

Lost within this world of mental abstraction, the sound of a door opening and soft steps slowly seeps into my awareness. Startled, I look up to see Jesse standing besides me. "Author" becomes protective, trying to keep her ideas from floating away. "Mother" aches to be with him. She smiles. Now the two parts of me blend. Two voices speak at once, the tone sounding strange to my ears.

"Jesse, I've got to write today. I must finish this book. I wish I could play with you but I can't. I love you, munchkin." "Mother's" voice is clearly audible now, as "Author" quietly slips away.

ENLIGHTENING IDENTITY

Each one of us is more than the one self we call Anne, Laura, Bill or David. We all have an array of personalities that appear and reappear at their respective times. I call these parts of the self "identities."[1] Because of our conditioning, many of our identities think, feel, perceive and act in ways that cause us discomfort or pain. Identities may be in either low- or high-frequency states of consciousness and in fact (depending on which identity is currently in control) determine the consciousness state we are in.

Transforming the consciousness of the whole personality involves learning to recognize and transform the consciousness of the particular identities that constitute the personality system. This entails becoming aware of the array of unenlightened identities that constitute the false self (conditioned persona).

Unenlightened identities are stuck in low-frequency states of consciousness. Ignoring the needs of the total body-mind-spirit, they selfishly like to run the whole show. Until we become awakened to these identities, we are unconscious and powerless over our conditioning, our states of consciousness and our lives. The price we pay

---

[1] Although I have traditionally seen these parts referred to as "subpersonalities," I have chosen to use the world "identity." It's the word I received in my training and it more accurately reflects my experience of them.

96

for this unconsciousness is the misery of feeling disconnected from higher power.

Enlightened identities are free of conditioning and are in high-frequency states of consciousness. They work in harmony with the total body-mind-spirit and express the individual's essence. The process of enlightening an identity involves helping this unenlightened aspect of ourselves lift out of its conditioning and lower states of consciousness and align itself with our divine nature.

In order for the *whole* personality to express its highest potential, our unenlightened identities must be enlightened. Enlightenment[2] happens in three steps:
- Disidentifying from conditioning — becoming an observer of the conditioned identity
- Understanding and embracing conditioning — acknowledging that conditioned limitations constitute the perfect opportunity for growth
- Healing or transforming conditioning — raising the consciousness of the identity so that it may align with higher consciousness

---

[2]Enlightenment is a relative term. Each of us is enlightened to some degree and unenlightened to some degree. We become more enlightened as we free specific identities from their conditioning. The turning point in the transformational process comes when the majority of our identities are no longer governed by their conditioning but are able to move consistently into alignment with the higher self. In other words, enlightenment is not something that happens to you after you become "perfect." Enlightenment is a process that involves the steady, step-by-step freeing of more identities, allowing them to reflect brightly the radiant light of your inner sun.

97

DISIDENTIFYING

As we have already discussed in Part 2, awakening to our highest potential begins as we learn to detach from the false self and increasingly align with the observer.

Exercise: Observing Identities

As in my example at the beginning of this section, notice the many different voices that constitute the person you call "you." You may do this by thinking of the variety of "roles" you play in your life. Are you a professional of some sort? If yes, then you have a "professional" identity that is different from the part of you that is a parent or that likes to play or be sexy or be creative. You may also focus on a number of emotional states you find yourself in. For example, when you are angry, ask the identity that is angry to come into your awareness. Then allow yourself to "feel" its presence or "see" its form. You may see an adult with clenched fists and jaw, or you may have a sense of a young child throwing a temper tantrum. All identities have a "role" they play within the context of the personality as well as an emotional overtone. See if you can get specific about these qualities. Ask yourself, "How does this identity behave, feel, think, perceive?" You may even want to jot the qualities down in a journal so you can work with them later. Sometimes it is handy to give each a name, but don't be too quick or rigid in labeling them. (Unenlightened identities are often caught in "roles" at first, but as they become more enlightened, they also become more fluid. So be careful about boxing yourself in with labels. It is more important to be with the thinking-feeling-sensation of the identity.) Don't let yourself get hung up by writing style or grammar.

Examples:

> *I pull my hair. Toss about. Pace.*
> *Thoughts of failure. Hard.*
> *Control. Nervous. Mental.*
> *Trying to figure out how to get out*
> *of dilemma. Old and worn.*
> *Possible name: Worrier*

> *Playful. Spontaneous laughter.*
> *Warm. Open. Love to touch and*
> *feel baby on skin. Sensual.*
> *Expressive. Curious. Full of*
> *wonder. Joyful. Young, mobile*
> *and flexible. A lot of movement.*
> *Possible name: Free Play*

> *Intense, driven. Highly motivated.*
> *Extremely focused. Don't stop to*
> *eat. Close self off. Ear plugs.*
> *Annoyed at interruptions. Closed.*
> *Protected. Hard and rigid.*
> *Maleness. Energy comes out of*
> *head like a force beam.*
> *Possible name: Get It Done*

> *Open. Peaceful. Compassionate.*
> *Soft. Caring. Expanded*
> *throughout field. Telepathic.*
> *Maybe psychic. Hypersensitive to*
> *feeling state but remain centered.*

> *Power.   Yielding.   Flexible.*
> *Female.   Cloaked in light.   Skirts.*
> *Flowing scarves.*
> *Possible name: Female Power*

Writing in this way helps you to become more aligned with your observer. It allows you to become a nonjudgmental observer of your set of characters. This in turn enables you to navigate with your awareness out of your conditioning and helps to strengthen your ability to work with and transform the unenlightened aspects of yourself. Once you have detached yourself from your identities, you can begin to understand and embrace them.

UNDERSTANDING AND EMBRACING UNENLIGHTENED IDENTITY

There are usually a number of identities that are "in charge" of the personality. These are the identities we feel most comfortable with. They constitute the persona we tend to think of as ourselves. For example, I tend to see myself as a creative person who takes charge of situations easily, is emotionally detached and is basically pleasant to be around without being overly polite. My husband, while practical and businesslike, identifies with being cordial, yielding and playful.

Because all of us tend to identify with some of our identities more than others, there are many identities within the whole range of the personality that have been denied or rejected by the "identities in charge." The denied identities usually stay hidden from view until something happens to activate them. Then, all of a sudden, we surprise ourselves — by losing our temper, by laughing uncontrollably, by saying something "so unlike us," by feeling unnerved or on edge. Many of these denied identities act in negative ways to get our attention and recognition. They want to be heard, just as a child who is being ignored by a parent will do something naughty to get the parent's attention.

101

I remember being shocked one afternoon when a long repressed "mean and nasty" part of myself became highly charged, directing all sorts of ugly, childish remarks toward a friend who had acted in a way that I did not like. When I sat down to work with this identity, I became aware of little mean men who were sick and tired of always feeling second to my "spiritual" parts. Let out of their cage, they raged and vented the nastiest phrases, much to the chagrin of my "spiritual" side.

Much of the healing work we do is simply that of listening and understanding. We must do this with all of our identities equally, being careful not to give preferential treatment to any one over the other. That means that both sets — those in charge and those denied — need to be listened to in a nonjudgmental and accepting fashion. Our identities are unenlightened until they come into alignment with our higher nature. Just because an identity is in charge (and comfortable) does not mean it is enlightened. An identity becomes enlightened when it functions in a high-frequency state of consciousness most of the time. There are plenty of low-frequency identities in charge of our personalities. (It is obvious that a low-frequency identity is in charge when we walk around angry or depressed. But there are also identities which are not as obviously unenlightened. For example, although I've grown to be comfortable with my emotional detachment, as I evolve I become increasingly aware of how unenlightened this identity is, of how this identity closes me off from feelings of love and joy. As more and more identities come into alignment with our higher nature, those that once "seemed" enlightened may come to seem unenlightened. The transformational process is one in which identities are lifted up into higher consciousness step by step.)

The process of understanding and embracing an identity involves being open to and accepting of the identity, even if we do not like it or it shames us. The way to achieve this understanding is to align with the observer. There will always be identities that are judgmental of others — as my "spiritual" identities were judgmental of my "mean men" and vice versa. The goal here is not to "make" these nonaccepting identities accepting. It is, rather, to navigate with our awareness into the accepting parts of ourselves — our observer and higher self. From this standpoint we can listen compassionately to all parts of ourselves equally. We hear the cries of desperation from those who have been hurt and abused; we hear the loud judgment of those who have abused; and we appreciate the motives, desires and special needs of each.

DIALOGUING

Dialoguing is a tool that helps you listen to and understand your identities. It is a way of accessing and communicating with the many parts of yourself that usually get lost in the general rumble of noise and clutter in your head. You may dialogue by writing down the viewpoint of each identity you are working with or by closing your eyes and sending and receiving thoughts, impressions and images.

If you decide to dialogue on paper, take your journal and a pen into a private area of your house. Regardless of whether you will be dialoguing on paper, give yourself ample time with no distractions in which to work. Get comfortable and close your eyes. If you have enough time, do the Daily Meditation and create your healing space. This will allow you to relax, feel safe and align yourself with your observer. It will also help to attune your brain, nervous system and circulatory system with higher consciousness. Breathe deeply into your abdomen, letting go of tension on each exhalation; then think of moving deeper and deeper into your center.

When you are feeling relaxed and in touch with your higher self, invite the identity that is presently activated to come into your awareness. Allow your mind to relax and become receptive to whatever impressions it receives. Some people get clear visual impressions of their identities. A hurting child may appear as a little blind girl or a little boy on crutches. A controlling identity may appear stiff and rigid. An angry rebel may appear thrashing about. I've worked with a variety, including dark, cloudlike forms, young girls in petticoats, shattered glass and monsters. Some people don't get a visual sense but perceive these identities as voices or sensations.[1]

The key to successful dialoguing is spontaneity. Don't censor, question or criticize your material. Just write and do it quickly. If you have trouble, you may have a strong censor identity or critical identity. Shift your focus from the identity you are working with to the identity blocking the dialogue. Ask, "Who are you and why are you blocking me?" Always work with what is most in your awareness at the time. For example, if your inner process is interrupted by a phone call and you find it difficult to get back to the work you were doing, then stop. Work with the identity that is having difficulty. Such opportunities can lead to very powerful healing sessions.

The easiest way to start dialoguing is to divide the dialogue between your observer and your identity. Your observer (Ob) may ask all sorts of questions of your identity (Id) or make appropriate comments.

Ob: Who are you?
Id: I am a sickness. I live inside your chest. I make you choke and want to puke. I am the putrid monster that loves to make your life look bleak.
Ob: Yes, I recognize you from the past. But why now? It's been so long since you've shown yourself to me.
Id: Because you're about to take a big, new step into the world, and I don't want you to. I want to hold you back.

---

[1]Two excellent books to read on the process of making contact with identities are Robert A. Johnson, *Inner Work* (New York: Harper & Row, 1986); and Hal Stone and Sidra Winkleman, *Embracing Our Selves* (San Rafael, CA: New World Library, 1985).

Once you've started a dialogue in this way, you may find a new voice (NV) spontaneously appearing. The new voice is often an identity that has a strong viewpoint on the present issue. Let it speak. It has come into the dialogue for a reason. Go with whatever spontaneously happens and your inner work will be richer.

Ob: So, you're the one who's been making me tired, who's been slowing me down, preventing me from finishing.

Id: Aha! (Smiling.) You've got it, honey.

Ob: I know. I can feel you in my heart and throat, stifling my love and creativity.

NV: I don't want you in my life! Go away! Stop tormenting me!

Sometimes you may find there is no observer present, only two conflicting identities. Fine. Go with what is happening and bring your observer in later during the healing.

NV: I want to feel good about work and love. Those pests get in the way. Get out of here! I hate you! You wreck my life! You make me miserable!

Pests: Yes, that is who we are — pests! Ha, ha. (They laugh and poke and pick at me.)

Ob: There is a war in here. I see a tormentor and tormentee. Let's bring in some light and see what happens.

The goal of dialoguing is discovery. If you write spontaneously, allowing the words to come forth from your unconscious, you will discover things about yourself you never knew.

I'm working with the light. A whole scenario unfolds: A lot of crying. Someone puts a mask over my face and tries to suffocate me. Fighting. Skirmish. I am a male and I am on an island. I have won the fight, have fought off the enemy, but my throat, chest and mouth have been wounded. I am weakened. I am too vulnerable.

Some of what you discover may hurt, but the hurt is temporary and will pass with healing. If approached with an attitude of open questioning and willingness to grow, everything you discover may be used for actualizing your highest potential.

Exercise: Dialoguing

Practice dialoguing with the identities you've already observed (see Observing Identities, pp. 98-99).

For best results, do your Daily Meditation and create your healing space. Align yourself with your observing center. Then invite each identity, one at a time, into your healing space. Allow yourself to get as much of an impression of the character, mood and feeling of an identity before you start. Once you feel you've made strong contact, open to what needs to happen. Become aware if this part of yourself has something it needs to express to you. If not, you may want to ask it questions such as, "Who are you?" "What purpose do you serve?" "How are you feeling?" or "Why are you hurting me?" Let the identity answer. Respond as you are guided.

ALIGNING IDENTITIES WITH HIGHER CONSCIOUSNESS

Identities have free will. That is, they can choose whether they wish to align with higher nature or not. You cannot make an identity change. The goal of healing is to give the identity *the option* to move into higher consciousness. You may do this by directing light-fire into the identity itself (to help it release conditioned mental, emotional and/or perceptual programming) or by sending light-fire into the corresponding bodily sensations.

Surrounding an Identity with Light

After you have completed dialoguing, amplify your awareness of the identity in whatever form it comes to you. Now think of surrounding the identity with light-fire. Become aware of your accompanying sensations, feelings and thoughts. Think of the fire consuming whatever low-frequency states of consciousness are activated. Let go of your thought, and experience what happens.

I think of light-fire enveloping the sweet little girls in starched clean frocks — the ones that needed to be liked by everyone. And then I invite them to speak.

108

Girls: We are empty, not even real. No power. No voice. Just an empty shell of who we once were.
Jane: Where is your energy? Is there any left?
Girls: No.

Girls disintegrate. In their place appear cosmic mother and father (more about these on pp. 139-141) to bring support and guidance.

Most identities will respond. Some will not. If an identity will not respond, allow it to be or ask it why it won't respond. Identities that have been denied or repressed may need a lot of time in which to express themselves before they will be ready to align with higher consciousness. This is especially true of abused or neglected identities. Once acknowledged, they may need to express pain and rage; they may need to be listened to again and again before they will yield to light. Keep the identity in light even if you see no immediate response.

Light has a way of gently soothing and loving. Any small progress on the part of an identity should be validated and supported. In time, even the most difficult identities will yield to light, just as the most difficult children will eventually yield to love. The key here is acceptance, gentle persuasion and persistence.

Working with Body Sensations

It is also possible to work with an identity through its corresponding body sensation. To do this, amplify your awareness of the identity and ask yourself, "Where do I feel this identity in my body?" Move with your awareness into the area and remain there for awhile — in the felt sense of it.[1] Explore the area thoroughly. Think of moving your sun into the body part, aligning the center

---

[1]For more information on exploring and working with body sensation for emotional and spiritual growth, see Eugene T. Gendlin, *Focusing* (New York: Bantam, 1981).

of the sun with the organizing center of the identity causing the discomfort. Blaze up the fire, and experience what happens as fire begins to consume low-frequency states of consciousness that are ready to be released.

> I feel sick. The energy is trapped and thick in my heart center and throat. Love and expression are bottled up, muddied. I become a little person and travel into the pain. It becomes mud and I can't breathe. I suffocate as I thrash around for life, waiting to be rescued. The mud clogs my nostrils and lungs. I am choking, suffocating. Will I die? Or will I be saved? I ask the light-fire to burn through the mud. I climb on a wooden raft and hold on for safety.

Most of the time you will have an experience of the space clearing as discomfort is released. When this happens, be sure to fill the cleared space with purified light-energy. If you do not, there is always the chance of low frequency refilling the emptied space.

> The raft floats amid the mud and light as they wage war. The fires become hotter, consuming the mud. This is a battle between light and dark, self and death. It seems that as I move outwardly to express self, I must fight the identities that wish to suffocate that expression.
> The muddied spaces open to receive the light. I stand up on the raft and beat my chest. I am proud, feeling daring and powerful.

Sometimes the light does not penetrate the spaces of your body. This probably means there is too much low-frequency consciousness for you to release all at once or that you are just not ready to release it. If this happens, acknowledge the block and keep working with it a little at a time, or leave it alone and come back to it later. You can also try working with the identity directly.

AN
IDENTITY-FREEING
SESSION

The following is an example of an "identity-freeing" session. Use it to help you understand the process more completely. But remember, every person and each situation are unique. What you do may not in any way resemble this example. Trust yourself and follow your instincts.

As I sit upstairs in my office writing, I hear thunder. Remembering the laundry that is hanging outside on the line, I run down to see if Gene has gotten it. He hasn't and it's too late. The rain is pouring down now, drenching the clean, almost dry clothes. I become filled with rage — an emotion definitely out of proportion to the situation. Returning upstairs, I try to continue working but can't. The anger is bothering me too much, so I put down my original writing project and proceed to work with what is up for me now. I begin the process by writing what I am presently feeling and thinking:

Rage, disgust, laundry is lost. All he had to do was be aware of the clouds to save it! I am furious at his lack of awareness. The laundry is ruined. We have to start it all over again. Lump in

111

chest. Aware of perception: things have to be done right, and he just doesn't do them right. There are stiff values of right and wrong. Things not working out the way they should fill me with disgust.

As I write I become disidentified with the rage and find myself entering into my observing center. Closing my eyes, I ask this identity to present itself to me. In my mind's eye, I do a visual run-through of what just happened. I see fists clenched and jerky movements as I stomp about the room.

I then become aware of the issue of "control." This identity needs to be in control and becomes enraged when it feels helpless. I give the identity a name, Angry Controller (AC), and begin to dialogue with her.

AC: I'm so pissed. The laundry smells bad when it gets rained on. I hung it up on the line so that it would smell good. And now it's ruined. We'll have to wash and hang it again. Goddamn it, Gene. You're in charge down there. You have no awareness about things.

Ob: Gene was unplugging the computer when the lightning started. Maybe he was doing other things as well. The kids aren't here, so his attention was probably focused on work, too.

AC: Things never go right. I feel so helpless. Raining on laundry makes me sick. It's his fault.

Ob: Seems like making it his fault is one way you don't have to feel so helpless.

AC: Yeah, I can't stand it when things don't go the way I intended.

Ob: Why not?

AC: Because I feel so powerless . . .

Ob: Over?

AC: Powerless over life.

Ob: Seems like there will just be times when you can't be in control.
AC: But I can't stand the feeling.
Ob: So you make yourself feel more powerful by getting angry and storming around.
AC: Yeah. I do feel more powerful that way.
Ob: (suggesting) Let's practice feeling powerless.
AC: Okay. I'll try.

I close my eyes and allow Angry Controller to reenact the events, this time feeling powerless. She throws up her hands and laughs for a moment but then turns to yell at Gene, "Why didn't you get the laundry?"

Ob: So, you can't stay feeling powerless for long?
AC: No. Guess not.
Ob: I think we need to do some lightwork.
AC: Yeah.

I become aware of the lump in my chest and choose to fill it with light rather than working with the identity directly. I navigate into the center of the lump. The pain increases as I become aware of a hurting. I am inside the lump. Now I want to cry. I blaze the light-fires into the lump as I explore it further. It feels messy and sticky. A voice from inside the lump calls, "Can't get out. Can't get out."
Someone is calling. Who is it? I see a little blind girl (LBG). She is crawling on the floor, lost, feeling around for something.

LBG: Nobody is helping me. I am all alone here. Blind. And no one helps me. It doesn't feel too good to be helpless. I will be trapped in here forever because no one is helping me. I

113

don't like it here. I want out. Someone help
me out.

Ob: Little helpless child, you are not alone. I
will help you. Let's bring in the light so you
may grow strong and see. How sad it feels
to be helpless. I know. I know. I
understand. I do.

She looks up, crying now. No one has ever
understood her. She has felt so alone. Only now
there is someone who understands. "Who are you?"
she asks.

Ob: I am you, little girl. I am the strong inner
core of you. You have the strength and the
will to help yourself. You are not alone. I
am a part of you.
AC: I'm not all alone or helpless?
Ob: No. With love you will rise and be free.

The little blind girl rises and looks around.
The lump is now radiating light. Angry Controller
and the little blind girl become one. "Gene doesn't
care! He wasn't loving! He didn't get the laundry.
The laundry is lost. I feel so lost."
Then, with new insight, "The laundry is my
lost self — with no one to save me (not even
Gene!)" Laugh. "So, that is why I was so furious
— no one was there to save the lost laundry.
Nobody cared for it! Nobody cared for me!"

Ob: Why the anger?
AC: It made me strong. I felt so weak, so sad, so
lost. My anger made me strong.
Ob: And now?
AC: I need to strengthen myself with love and
light. I don't need anger or Gene to save
me. I must save myself.
Ob: And the laundry?

AC: That's so silly! The laundry is laundry —
that's all. It got left in the rain — that's all.
Maybe it likes the feel of rain drops on its
surface. Maybe it likes to play in rain. Let
the laundry be. Take care of my lost self.

When I do this work, I first magnify my union with
my higher self and ask for guidance. I then work
spontaneously with whatever comes up. In the preceding
example, I was guided to dialogue with Angry Controller.
I then became aware of a prominent bodily sensation — a
lump in my chest — and intuitively made the choice to
direct light into that rather than directly into the identity.

As soon as light was directed into the lump, a voice
from within the lump spoke. I had no idea she was there
until I started writing. As I wrote, her presence became
clearer. This is a pointed example of the relationship
between body sensation and identity. There is always a
relationship, although we are often unaware of it.

At a point in the process it became clear to me that
Angry Controller and the little blind girl were one and the
same identity. It is often the case that anger protects a
wounded or frightened identity.

The most important part of this inner work for me
was seeing the lost laundry as a projection of my lost
little blind girl, my lost child. Often before we do this
kind of healing, the parts of our identity we've
"disowned" or repressed are projected out onto external
people or things. Channeling light reveals this projection
and helps us reintegrate the identity back into ourselves.

HARMONIZING

Identities at war within us create a great deal of our suffering. If one identity is afraid of risk but another dreams of adventure, we are in conflict. Neither identity gets what it needs because the opposing identity is working against it. If one identity is lonely and yearns for companionship but another is afraid of being vulnerable, we're in conflict. Again, neither part can be satisfied because of the opposition. From a higher perspective, all that *is* functions harmoniously in oneness. There is no separation. Suffering is caused by the illusion of separateness resulting from unenlightened programming. Lifting our identities into high-frequency consciousness will help them to utilize their energy to benefit the whole personality and to harmonize with one another so as to support the unique purpose and needs of each.

Exercise: Healing and Harmonizing[1]

Do the Daily Meditation and prepare your healing space. Ask your higher self to make its presence known to you and to participate in the work that follows.

Ask each of two identities that are in conflict to reveal itself to you separately. From your observing center, begin a dialogue with one, then the other. You may ask such questions as, "Why

---

[1]School of Actualism, used with permission.

are you acting that way?" or "Is there anything you need to tell me?" Write spontaneously, allowing whatever comes into your awareness. Do this with each identity until the process feels complete. You will often find that conflicting identities have unexpressed hostility. This needs to be expressed before you begin lightwork.

After each identity has been heard, direct light-fire into the identity or its corresponding bodily sensations. Do this by thinking of the sun surrounding the identity or aligning with the bodily discomfort. Then think of the sun turning into a ball of flame.

Your higher self now turns toward one identity, asking it what it needs for healing. When the identity responds, higher self gives the identity what it asks for. The same question is asked of the other identity, and its needs are filled. The fire continues to consume what is ready to be released by the identities. When you feel a lift, think of the fire coming to a halt. Ask each identity to open to the purified light-energy pouring back in.

Input from higher self in combination with the harmonizing properties of light is a very powerful way of bridging inner discord. Higher self, which is always unconditionally loving, can give you and the identity insight into its unique purpose within the personalty. As each identity opens to its own purpose and simultaneously hears the purpose of the other, harmonizing takes place.

LESSON LEARNING

Our conditioning provides an endless opportunity for growth and expansion. Each time we free a conditioned identity, we learn a lesson. We make enormous strides in our ability to awaken to our highest potential.

Recently, I received an invitation from a prestigious hospital to give a talk on my recovery from bulimia. I was to be paid very well for something that would take no more than an hour of my time and very little preparation. I was thrown into the worst indecision I'd been in in years. "Why not do it?" I asked myself, "What's to lose?" And yet there was another part of me that just did not want to make the trip.

One identity really "got off" on the glamor — the money, the prestige, the jetting about. The other identity did not want my energy diverted away from inner development, creativity and transformational work with others. This part was also aware that I was prepared to tell a partial truth. I would talk about my recovery from every conceivable angle except the one I discuss in this book — the transforming power of inner light-fire — in order not to appear too "far out" to the professionals in the audience. It was no longer interested in going along with this kind of lie.

As I worked with these identities, listening to their needs and filling them with light, I felt a powerful coming together as I realized I could satisfy both needs

— to go, have fun, make money *and* remain centered in my full truth. The lesson learned was that I could no longer speak partial truths. I was going to have to find a way to communicate the powerful role light-energy played in my recovery process. With this realization came a sense of expansion.

As the self expands, the lesson learning process takes us into new arenas. We are often catapulted into what feels like frightening challenges. But fear is only a conditioned response to what is new. As we raise the consciousness of the personality, we may leverage our identity into the excitement of the unknown and into the peace of higher wisdom.

The work of identity transformation must take place in an open, flexible and creative inner environment. The process is fluid, unfolding in a myriad of intricate patterns. Our greatest success comes as we learn to listen to the self — to the voices of the many identities within and to the highest wisdom from our divine inner nature.

FOLLOWING HIGHER DIRECTION

Before awakening to light, my actions for the most part were motivated by conditioned programming: fear, rebellion, self-centeredness and unmet needs for love, nurturance, security and power. In my early twenties I chose to work nights, not because I was higher directed but because I had identities within me that were afraid of interrelating with daytime employees. I earned $6 an hour, yet when my boss offered to make me the night supervisor with increased salary, I turned him down. This decision was based on fear, not on higher guidance.

What is higher direction, and how can we tell the difference between it and the many voices of our unenlightened identities? Higher direction is the way we understand our higher power's wish for us. It is hearing, feeling or sensing the highest frequency option for us at any particular time in our lives. Following higher direction always results in the most optimal outcome. It leads to the greatest good for all involved and brings feelings of peace, well-being and harmony.

When we act from an unenlightened identity, another part of us usually still questions whether this is the right decision, thereby fostering a residual sense of unrest and unsettledness. Perhaps we have plunged forward in haste, fearing that we may lose out forever if we don't act right now, or perhaps we have made the decision in such a giddy, wildly excited state of mind that no counterview ever had a chance of being heard. Whatever the consciousness we act from, conditioning-governed decisions often carry with them a vague sense of unease or impending regret.

Until we've done the work of disidentifying from and transforming our conditioned programming, it is very difficult to know whether we are following higher guidance or not. Our minds are often enveloped in the din of constant "chatter," a disturbing form of inner noise pollution. Because so much of the personality is still driven by unenlightened identity, it is difficult to discern the nature of the different voices. The needs of the unenlightened identities are so pronounced, and often so loud, that they drown out the small quiet voice of higher self. As we do the work of transforming personality identity, the chatter fades and the quiet voice within becomes more and more apparent.

Exercise: Discovering Higher Direction

Become quiet. Move into your upper room, and think of radiant consciousness moving throughout your body and field. Downpour the light throughout your body, and then expand your sun around your field. Move with your awareness back into your upper room, as this is the area that is most open to communication from higher self.

Hold a question in your mind. For example, "Should I buy a new home?" or "Is this the right time to make a career change?" Think of each option, one at a time, that is available to you. Hold the first option in the light. Notice what happens. Does it get stronger? Or does it seem to fade away? Do the same with all other options. What happens to them? This method will give you a clear indication as to which option holds up stronger in the light. Follow this option.

If you become aware of a negative reaction (such as doubt or fear) activated by the decision, work with the identity behind that reaction. As you work with the identity, discover what doubts, fears, rage or other low-frequency conditioning is motivating it and why. Then hold it in light-fire to help it release low-frequency consciousness and open to high-frequency consciousness. Many identities have unmet power, security and love needs which they try to get met by making demands that don't serve the whole personality. When held in light these identities often experience their own inner sense of power, security and love and may be willing to let go of the outcomes they once thought were necessary. When this happens — and only when this happens — are you free to act according to higher direction, not according to the desires of your unenlightened identities.

Let's look at an example of how this process works. Suppose you need to decide whether to accept a transfer to another city. The new position pays $10,000 more a year, but you love your home and don't want to leave it or the community you now live in. What should you do?

Begin with the Daily Meditation. This will put you in the optimal place in consciousness for making a higher-directed decision. Set the stage by asking, "What decision will bring the highest good to all involved?" Move with your awareness into your upper room.

Now pose the question, "Should I move or should I stay?" Hold the first option in the light, visualizing yourself at your new position in the new city. What happens? Does it gain in power or diminish? Do the same with the second option. Visualize yourself staying where you are. Does the light cause it to increase or decrease in power? If you need to, move back and forth between the two. Can you sense a difference, even a subtle one? Once you have a felt sense of which option will be the most powerful for you, make the decision. If you decide on the second option, say out loud, "I decide to stay here and give up the $10,000 a year." What happens as you hear yourself say the words? Are there any doubts? If so, then ask the identity that is doubting to come into your awareness so you can start dialoguing with it.

You can begin by saying, "It seems that the decision to stay here feels more powerful when I hold it in the light. Why don't you want to go along?" Perhaps the identity will say, "We could do so much with $10,000. How can you give it up?" Continue your dialogue until you understand completely why this part of you is objecting to the decision. Let's pretend the dialogue proceeds like this:

Ob: It feels like the decision to stay here will lead to greater opportunity in the long run.
Id: But I'm so afraid to make the wrong decision.
Ob: Why?
Id: Because we have in the past. We've made decisions that have hurt us.
Ob: How?
Id: Remember the time . . .
Ob: Yes. We did make a decision that lost us money, but we learned a valuable lesson and the money wasn't as important as the lesson we learned.
Id: But I don't want us to lose more money. I'm scared we won't be able to send the kids to college and build the dream house.
Ob: What good would a dream house do in a place we don't even like?
Id: I know. But at least we'd be safe.
Ob: Let's do some lightwork.

After you have uncovered this identity's fear of losing financial security, hold the identity in the light and ask it to release its fear. Stay with this until you feel a release. Then ask the identity to receive the light-energy pouring back in. Now make the decision again. Say, "I decide to stay here in this home that I love and give up the $10,000 a year." Notice if there are any more doubts. If there are, keep working as before until you have cleared out all opposition to the decision.

You may find that as you work, an identity may show you something that indicates you have made the wrong decision. An identity's fear of loss may uncover a genuine concern. In the preceding example, holding the identity's fear of losing financial security in the light may have revealed a centered place of cautious wisdom. The actual role of this identity may have been to bring to your attention an unlighted tendency on your part to act hastily. When this happens, you then may need to work with the original identity's strong desire to stay. Is it afraid of the unknown? Is it afraid of failure? Continue working with all identities until you are sure without a doubt that you have made the right decision.

Hold the decision in the light. If it gains in intensity and power and there is no more inner opposition, then do it. If it fades in the light, no matter what reasons you can find for doing it, let it go.

Be aware that after you have made a firm, "final" decision, you are likely to be tested with some new development. New layers of as-yet-unprocessed anxiety, confusion or greed may well come up in the next few days, and you may have to repeat the whole process. Although this process takes time, compare the investment of another hour's time to losing thousands of dollars a year or to being stuck in a place where you are miserable.

Another way to be sure you are following higher guidance is to check in directly with your higher self.

Exercise: Meeting Your Higher Self

Do the Daily Meditation, paying special attention to align your brain with the radiant awareness of your upper room. Ask your brain to soften into its actual design as a receiving station for your higher mind.

Return to your upper room and visualize an inner chamber of light. Notice there are stairs that lead up to a special area of the chamber in which your higher self resides. Slowly climb the stairs, and as you do, notice that the spaces of your body become less and less dense as you attune to higher and higher states of consciousness.

When you are inside this chamber, ask your higher self for feedback on any question you may have. Do not try to force a response. Remain as relaxed as you can, and wait for impressions to filter into your awareness.

After you do this, you may want to work with any identity that opposes the insight acquired in this way by following the directions outlined in the previous exercise.

Guidelines for Following Higher Direction

Do the Daily Meditation.

Ask your higher power to guide you in making the decision which will bring the highest good for all involved.

Hold your options in the light. Choose the option that seems most strong and powerful when held in the light.

Say the decision out loud, and notice your doubts, fear and other adverse reactions to the decision.

125

Dialogue with the identities that oppose the decision. Discover what unmet needs are motivating them.

Surround these identities in light, and ask them to release low-frequency states of consciousness into the fire and open to light-energy pouring back in.

If after you have held an identity in the light and it has released its low-frequency states of consciousness, its opposition to your decision holds strong, work with the identity that was responsible for your original decision to discover if there are any low-frequency states of consciousness motivating it.

Continue to work in this way until you no longer have any opposition to the decision you've chosen.

Check out your final decision by holding it in the light. If it remains strong and there is no more doubt or fear, then do it!

If your firm decision begins to waver in a few days, do the process again until you get it to hold steady.

PART FOUR

INNER CHILD
INNER VISION

"It's not knowing who I am; it's being so busy with things — doing, doing, doing — all the time for others. And then I wait for the gratitude, but it never comes, and I get so upset that I eat. Why am I sacrificing myself? I'm bored and restless and so out of touch. I feel so empty, like a shell. And it's beginning to actually hurt when I hear myself offer to do things for people." As Anne speaks, I notice her hands nervously pulling on her dress, crumpling it in her hand. Her pasted smile is faintly visible, like a shadow at dusk. She is clearly agitated as she shifts her focus from one area of the room to the other. I can feel her pain all bottled up inside, and I know she needs to let herself contact a real place of feeling.

"Okay, let's do some healing. Close your eyes and breathe deep . . . deep . . . deeper. Move with your awareness into the radiance of your healing space — full of light and higher power's infinite love and wisdom."

Silence as we both relax into this safe and warm environment. *"Now invite the bored, restless part of you into this space for healing. Let her know that in this place nothing will be taken from her. She is safe here."*

Time expands. Moments lengthen, and we enter the inner time of healing. *"Go into the pain, Anne, right into the center of the pain."*

"She's a child . . . in the playpen. She can't get out. She's angry and very hurt. She cries for food because it's better than being trapped in there alone." Anne's face distorts. The agitation moves from her hands to her upper chest. She begins to cry.

"What does she need?"

"Love. She wants to come out and be held . . . . I am picking her up. She likes this . . . . Now she's becoming stiff like she's not sure she really wants to stay. She's afraid."

"Of what?"

"I don't know." Silence. Her forehead wrinkles, trying to understand. Then, with a knowing nod, *"She's*

afraid that if she lets herself enjoy the love, I'll stop holding her."

"Is that true? Can you hold her forever?"

Laugh. "No. I'd like to put her down, but she seems scared. She's clutching me now — afraid of this new environment, of the unknown. She's clutching my leg and skirt."

"Ask her what she wants from you."

"She wants to be played with — loved."

"Can you do that?"

"Yes, I can read, draw — and she would like that."

"Okay, now fill her with the light. Blaze up the fire to consume everything she is ready to let go of. Ask her to release her fears and whatever else is ready to go into the flames."

More tears. "The playpen is gone, but she has a pacifier and she won't let it go. She wants to but is afraid of being alone. She needs her pacifier to keep her safe."

"She can keep it," I say softly. "This is not the time to let it go."

We are quiet for a long while. Inner space is reshuffling; so is future potential. "Now feel the dynamic action of the sun filling her with light."

A smile.

"She and I are hugging. I've tied the pacifier around her neck so she'll have it when she needs it. I'm throwing the crackers and sugar, the fear of being alone, into the fire. I can't ever be alone. I have the Holy Spirit and I have my child. We all have each other. I'll never be alone!"

DIVINE CHILD

As babies we had infinite potential, which our parents had the responsibility of nurturing. Perhaps they did a good job.   Perhaps they didn't. Regardless, now it is our turn. Inside us is a divine child who possesses the vision and potential for all that is beautiful and valuable.   That child aches to express himself or herself in the world. It is up to us to give that child a chance.

If we do not experience joy, serenity and vitality, our potential lies dormant. We must learn to honor the child who loves to play, create, laugh and be silly, to be enthralled with the power of his or her own little voice, to jump, run, hop and fall. This child needs expression. Perhaps not in the same way as a child of three or six or eight, but in his or her own precious way, the child needs to be heard and felt.

Many of us disconnect from our inner child in an attempt to live in the "real" world. I never wanted to grow up because I didn't want to leave the wonders of my world for an adult world that seemed empty, drab and dull. My child yearned to stay with me but was lost amidst the forces of a society that threatened to smother her. Years later I discovered her within the wreckage of my young adult years. I had to wade through the muddy layers that suffocated her, crying out in pain and grief as I felt her loss. As I poked and dug, uncovering her near-lifeless form, and as I slowly nurtured her back to health, my life changed. No longer imprisoned by the phantom images of adult roles and rules, she slowly came to life.

As I let her dream once again and took her dreaming seriously, she added enormous creativity, vitality and purpose to my life. My inner vision became not a plaything to put on hold while I went about the business of acting in the dull real world but a seed to water and nurture to fruition until every minute of my day was infused with the inner spirit of my essence.

What are your visions? Your dreams? What in your wildest imagination would you love to make or do for yourself right now? Let your child dream, and just as a three-year-old acts out through make-believe, you can act out in this world we call "reality," making yourself and others believe in your inner truth. Your child is your essence, the seed of all your dreams, creativity, spontaneity and joy. If you ignore the child, you ignore your spirit. If you kill the child, you kill your spirit. If you stifle the child, you stifle your spirit. If you nurture and honor the child, you nurture and honor your spirit.

ILLUMINE THE PAST CHANGE THE NOW

No matter what our childhood, no matter how we were raised, it is possible to heal the inner child with inner light. Light comes from a divine source. Its impact exists outside of time/space. Only our physical lives manifest in past, present and future. The illusion of personality is that the past is over. From personality's perspective, this is true. What was done to us is over and cannot be redone. But from the timeless perspective of our own infinite godliness, we live in our past, present and future all at once. What happened once happens now, and as we illumine the past, we change the now. Bring light-fire into childhood memory and alter the potential of your future. Bring light-fire into old wounds and hurts. Allow it to consume the rage, the sadness and the grief of the times you were not heard, validated or supported. Feel the Mother/Father God within sending love and support to nurture your ailing lost child.

Ultimately, we can only look within to be loved unconditionally. No one, not even Mom or Dad, can do this for us. They had their own weaknesses, challenges and conditioning to contend with and sometimes could not be there for our needs. As adults, with a divine heritage, we can find that inner source of mother/father love and support. We are, in our connection with the creator, capable of supplying our personality creation with all the love and nurturance we need for survival and growth. Learning to make contact with the great cosmic mother/father within has powerful healing potential. With this kind of unconditional loving, we can nurse our ailing child back to health. With light, we penetrate the dark overlays of conditioning that have held the child captive. With light-fire, we consume the conditioning to set the child free. With love and support from cosmic mother/father, we give the child the strength and confidence to believe in himself or herself. And again with light, we enable the child to feel his or her own inner source of power and radiance. As the inner child grows and expresses outwardly, our visions and dreams become our reality, the boundaries between work and play diminish and joyful laughter permeates our world.

FREEING THE VULNERABLE CHILD

For many of us the work of contacting the inner child can be painful because we have to peel off the layers of conditioning that have severed our child from us. If we come from families in which our needs were not met, we must face the pain of those unmet needs once more.[1] For those of us who come from dysfunctional families, some of our inner child work entails grieving the loss of our unmet needs. Light brings the awareness of this loss to the surface. As light penetrates the darkness, the vulnerable child within is revealed. As we direct light into the pain and grief of the loss, the soothing effect of inner light eases the hurt. As we continue to throw all rage, anger, grief and hurt into the light-fire, the essence held within is returned to the child, giving him or her inner love, power and strength with which to satisfy needs and rebuild dreams and visions.

Inner child work frees us as adults from conditioned defenses that once served to protect our vulnerability.

---

[1] The basic needs of children are security (food, clothing, shelter, health care); to be held and touched; encouragement and praise; stimulation (challenge, fun, play); structure (limits and boundaries); to be taken seriously and respected; to be allowed to be different; to feel wanted; and to have feelings validated. For more information, see John Bradshaw, *Bradshaw on the Family* (Deerfield Beach, FL: Health Communications, 1988) and *Healing the Shame That Binds You* (Deerfield Beach, FL: Health Communications, 1988). Also see Charles L. Whitfield, M.D., *Healing the Child Within* (Deerfield Beach, FL: Health Communications, 1987).

When we are hurt repeatedly as children, we build a wall or defense to protect us from further hurt. Although this wall serves to protect the tiny, helpless, vulnerable child from feeling more hurt, it also serves to protect the child from deep feelings such as love, tenderness, caring, compassion and intimacy. As these walls are built, we lose touch with our spontaneity and creativity as well. So although the child needs these walls to ensure emotional survival, the adult (who is no longer helpless) needs to tear down these walls in order to achieve greater depths of intimacy and creativity.

As we bring the light-fire into the personality system, these walls or defenses are revealed and consumed, releasing energy again back to child-essence and bringing more intimacy, depth of feeling, creativity and spontaneity into our lives. As we awaken to our divine potential, we become again as children.

We love innocently.

We create passionately.

We play wildly.

Vision, dream and reality blend together as we walk in the world that we create for ourselves.

PROTECTING THE VULNERABLE CHILD

Our vulnerable child can be easily hurt. This child needs to be loved, cared for and supported and is highly sensitive to any form of rejection or abandonment. The vulnerable child is responsible for our tenderness and our deep feelings of intimacy.

In our culture, we usually protect this child early in life by denying or disowning him or her. When our child is hurt, we may get angry instead of registering the hurt or we may retreat from relationships into work. The vulnerable child is never present in business relationships and, sadly, is rarely present in most intimate relationships where his or her special gift of loving is so badly needed. As we learn to open to this exquisitely sensitive part of ourselves, we must learn how to protect it in a way that does not deny it. We need this child for deep emotional relationships. But just as a child who loves to play all day may not know how to make a living and a child who is sensitive may not know how to stand up for himself or herself in abusive situations, the child needs to trust that the adult self will provide parenting. The inner child has to learn how to function in harmony with the more responsible adult parts of the self.

The key point here is to allow for balance within the personality. As we discover more and more of our child and allow that child to express through us, we will want to do it in a context of wholeness, with higher self overseeing the whole of our personality needs. Our higher self, while unconditionally loving, possesses the wisdom necessary to keep abreast of the specific needs of the personality at specific times. Thus, if the wild, imaginative, child part of us wants to do nothing but write children's stories, we are wise to check in with higher self for timing. Higher wisdom may tell us, "Yes, write children's stories in your spare time, but do not quit your job just yet," or "You have enough savings to last a year. Now is the time to dedicate yourself full time to writing children's stores." If the vulnerable child is so sensitive she falls apart at every critical glance, we need to develop what I call the inner warrior. I like to think of my inner warrior as a facet of my higher self that protects my soft, vulnerable parts with a light-shield. The shield protects by allowing only high-frequency states of consciousness into my body and field. Low-frequency states of consciousness are caught and consumed by the fires guarding the rim of my energy field.

Exercise: Creating a Light-Shield[1]

Do the Daily Meditation.

Expand your sun to surround your field. Move with your awareness out to the rim of your field. Notice if you feel or sense any of your energy leaking out beyond the rim. If you do, gently guide this part of you back inside. Now let yourself explore the rim, traveling around the circumference with your awareness. Are there any holes or openings? Is it well sealed? Wherever you find a break in the rim, think of sewing or patching it, and then seal it over with light. Once all the openings have been sealed, intensify the light on the rim. You may want to experiment with a few layers of light or one hard layer containing light-fire within the space of your field to see what works best for you.

---

[1] School of Actualism, used with permission.

This light-fire shield serves the same function as the defense mechanisms we built as children to protect us from hurt. The difference is that now we build the shield with awareness and in such a way as to protect us from low-frequency states of consciousness while allowing our full range of feeling and sensitivity to remain intact. The child who withdraws to guard against an abusive parent is very different from the adult who can shield with light and transform the residual victim consciousness. Once consciousness is raised, we can choose our response (rather than unconsciously reacting and defending our position) by "tuning in" to higher knowing for actual direction.

When you are in a situation in which you are being verbally attacked, think of blazing up the fires within your field to consume the low-frequency consciousness coming at you. Unify with the attacking person's higher self. You may also try to make contact with his or her vulnerable child. Some people project anger outward as a way of protecting their own vulnerable child. If you can help them to contact this deep place within themselves by disarming their defenses,[2] their need to direct anger at you will no longer be present.

---

[2]An excellent book on this subject is Jordan and Margaret Paul, *Do I Have To Give Up Me To Be Loved By You?* (Minneapolis: CompCare, 1983).

CREATING A SAFE AND NURTURING ENVIRONMENT

My vulnerable child did not show herself to me until I had created a safe and nurturing inner environment, until there was enough unconditional love present within me to hold her in my inner arms and warm her and soothe her hurts. This unconditionally loving part of myself, my cosmic mother/father, has the uncanny ability to cradle, nurture and caress whatever is hurting me. Whether I've acted in a way that I regret or whether someone else has hurt me, if I close my eyes and open to the love available to me from this part of myself, my wounds are easily soothed.

I like to think of cosmic mother/father as the archetypal mother/father that we all have imprinted within us. Even if we've never experienced a loving childhood, we possess a mind capable of calling forth an archetype/image of a nurturing parent. We can use the power of this archetype to give to our inner child all he or she needs and wants. Not to use this universal energy is to lose out on a powerful source of inner love and healing.

Exercise: Meeting Your Cosmic Mother/Father

Begin with the Daily Meditation and create your healing space.

Become aware that your higher self is with you and that you are surrounded in a crystalline white light as you prepare to take this journey together.

Your healing space now turns into a beautiful meadow or beach. You are a very young child playing with friends. You feel free, joyous and safe. Notice your higher self here with you — watchful, protective and loving.

As you play you become aware that two people are approaching. As they come into view, you recognize your mother and father. How does their presence affect how you feel and what you do? How does it affect your sense of safety? Your sense of joy? Your sense of freedom? How do you greet them? Do you run up to them or stay back? Do you hug them or not? Do you wish to share your activities with them? Do you introduce them to your friends?

What are their reactions to you? Do they want to be included?

Remember, this place is your healing space. You are in control and you have power, even if you are only a child. Now allow yourself to tell your parents how you feel about them being here. Remember you are safe and protected by your higher self and the light. Your parents cannot talk back to you and cannot harm you. In this fantasy they can only listen.

Tell your parents how you would like them to be. Let them know now what you have always needed from them. This is your time to say what you've always wanted to say and to be heard.

When you are done, notice that your higher self is now walking toward your dad, stepping within his spaces and aligning with him. Become aware of what happens as he is transformed into your cosmic father, the father you have always needed and wanted. Allow yourself to be still and feel the presence of this male being who is totally accepting of you. How do you relate? How do you feel about his presence here within your healing place? What special qualities does he now possess and give to you? Experience yourself change as you open to receive his special gifts.

Observe your higher self going over to your mom and aligning with her. Become aware of what happens as she is transformed into your cosmic mother, the mother you have always needed and wanted. Allow yourself to be still and feel the presence of this female being who is totally accepting of you. How do you relate? How do you feel about her presence here within your healing place? What special qualities does she now possess and give to you? Experience yourself change as you open to receive her special gifts.

Take a few moments to acknowledge your gifts and send love and gratitude back to your higher self, your cosmic father and cosmic mother. Make a promise to each that you will take these gifts with you into the world. As you wave goodbye for now, know that your cosmic parents will always be there for you whenever you call on them.

LIGHT CHILD

The vulnerable child held within the warmth of inner light grows to learn of his or her own inner resources and power. At first the child is dependent on the love of the cosmic mother/father, the inner parents. But slowly this child learns to build a powerful light-shield and finds inner strength. Now the child, still soft and yielding, still exquisitely sensitive and open, is touched by others and touches others with tenderness and compassion. Now inner love lessens the child's dependence on others for nurturance. Less vulnerable to pain, now functioning in higher frequency consciousness than before, this light child expresses its feelings, needs, desires, hopes and visions spontaneously and joyously.

Exercise: Healing the Vulnerable Child

Do the Daily Meditation and create your healing space.

Invite your child identity into this space and begin dialoguing with him or her. The child may need some coaxing, as children are shy. Be patient, allowing yourself to be with the child in whatever way is necessary. Your child may need to cry, grieve, ache or throw a fit. Let your child know that any action or behavior is okay with you. Allow your child to fully express her feelings and needs before you begin channeling light. So much of what hurts as a child is not being heard or supported. When your child has said all he or she needs to say, you may want to invite your cosmic mother, cosmic father or higher self to give your child the love, support and guidance he or she needs. Simultaneously, think of surrounding your child in light-fire, allowing him or her to release low-frequency states of consciousness and open to pure high-frequency energy.

HEALING THE PAST

Much of our present reality is affected by identities trapped in patterns set up in childhood. One way to free these identities is to go to the source of the patterning. The following exercise will free many identities in one large sweep. It is so powerful that I recommend you not do it more than once every three days.

Exercise: Time Machine[1]

Begin with the Daily Meditation.

Bring your sun to your navel and expand it throughout your field. Ask your higher self to reveal the experiences that are ready to be processed right now in order for you to gain a deeper understanding and acceptance of your childhood.

Think of yourself seated in a time machine. Become aware that your personality and your higher self are seated together within it. Your time machine begins to spin clockwise, moving back in time to the moment of your conception. What was the state of consciousness of your parents? Was there love and joy, or was there anxiety, fear, distrust or anger? Allow yourself to register and validate whatever impressions come into your awareness.

---

[1] Adapted from the school of Actualism with permission.

Now let yourself relive your gestation. Become aware of the enormous activity taking place as cells multiply and organs form. What are you conscious of? Is this a joyful time? What is the state of consciousness of your mother? Is she pleased with her pregnancy, or is she fearful and anxious? Does she want you inside of her? Does she want you as a baby? What sounds are you aware of? Do you feel healthy, or are toxic substances interfering with your sense of well-being? What is being communicated to you about life?

Now experience your birth. Are you fully conscious or drugged? Is your mother fully conscious or drugged? Are there problems with your birth? How are you received? How does it feel leaving the warm dark womb to come out into the world?

Move forward in time. Ask your time machine to stop at the memory of an event that powerfully impacted your childhood. Become aware of the details of this incident. Become aware of how your attitude toward life is being influenced. Are other people involved? If so, can you sense any attitudes they have that will affect your childhood?

Now become aware that your higher self is standing with you at this event. Experience your higher self's attitudes and feelings about this event. Higher self turns toward your child and asks the child what he or she needs. Experience as higher self gives your child what he or she needs. Higher self now turns toward your adult self and asks what you need. Experience as higher self gives you exactly what it is you need. Higher self now gives you a new understanding of the gifts and lessons present in this event. How can you benefit from this? Surround this event in healing, white, purifying energy.

Move back in time to the moment before conception. Think of your white sun spinning counterclockwise. Think of all the painful events, feelings, distorted attitudes and perceptions that you are now willing to release being caught up in the vortex of your spinning sun. As you move into the present, your higher self pulls those loads through your time tunnel. Think of your white sun spinning counterclockwise, suctioning out debris from the past, pulling it forward, into the present and out into your field to be processed by the purifying energy. Blaze up the consuming fire, allowing the debris which has been brought forward out of your time tunnel to be processed.

After you have experienced the loads being transmuted by the fire, move back down your time tunnel to the moment before conception. Think of your sun spinning in a clockwise direction and moving forward, depositing life-enhancing energy into the cleared spaces until the sun eventually returns to the present. Think of your sun becoming still.

Ask higher self to give you an experience of what you can do now to change the conditioning patterns set up in childhood so that they no longer continue to affect your life. Turn to your higher self and offer thanks for any new insights gained. Ask your higher self to step behind you, placing its hands on your shoulders, then stepping into your physical body and aligning. Relate intimately to higher self with all areas of your body. Ask your body to open fully to assimilate high-frequency light-energy pouring in.[2]

---

[2] The full range of techniques for healing the inner child cannot possibly be covered in this book. I am presently working on a more fully developed model for using inner light to heal the inner child.

PARTING WORDS

There is no doubt that we are entering an age of great planetary crisis. The questions that many of us now ask are, "How will we safely make the transition into the new century? How will we keep our planet alive and healthy? How can our planet become, once again, a safe home for ourselves and our children?" At the same time, we are increasingly aware of the dysfunction in our personal lives and our society at large. The task of saving our planet is integrally related to the task of saving our own emotional and spiritual lives. For some of us, the beginning stages of healing are self-centered. We become so wrapped up in our personal dramas that we may be blind to the larger perspective.

At some point, we must realize that our misery is but a speck in a real drama of unprecedented magnitude that is unfolding on the stage of the world. Humanity is facing choices today that will affect the life and well-being of every creature on the planet. For some of us, this realization brings with it a state of overwhelming despair. But it may help to know that although our misery is but a speck, we are not. Each of us has power to affect the destiny of our planet by the states of consciousness we maintain and by our actions. Planetary healing begins with personal healing. As each of us evolves personally, we become imbued with the awareness of oneness — that who I am and how I act have far-reaching effects on the whole of humanity. The healing process that takes us further into the core of ourselves paradoxically leads us away from the narcissism of self-involvement. As we take the time to heal our wounds, we become more and more aware of the hurt these personal wounds have caused us to inflict on others. We understand with compassion how the wounded in turn unconsciously act cruelly against life on our planet.

It is only with love that we heal our own hurts. Likewise, it is only with love that we enter into a healing relationship with our beloved planet Earth. A journey that may begin for some, as it did for me, as an intense love/hate affair with self to the exclusion of larger perspectives inevitably takes us so deeply inside that we eventually find the center that unifies each of us with the whole. As we contact our essence, we find the unique part we play in the drama of the whole. As we each become connected to our source, we cannot help but feel intimately connected to the whole of humanity and the planet.

My life once held more darkness than light. It took years for my small point of light to grow into an ever-brightening sun until there are now only points of darkness, little holes that crop up once in a while, holes that need to be climbed into, explored and filled with light.

My life today is one of surrendering to higher power. In my surrender, I become a channel of light and allow life process to weave its perfect pattern. And although I cannot know the form of destiny, there is one thing I do know — that working with light is a way of surrender, a way to higher wisdom, love and creativity. Once in touch with this, it is up to us to act so that our lives and the life of the planet may fulfill their greatest potential.

The work of personal fulfillment, spiritual growth and planetary service is ultimately the same. As we release the false conditioning that blocks our experience of greater joy, we open to a deep love and compassion for humanity that call us to service. The more we give, the more we receive. The more we receive, the more we wish to give. There is no limit to the abundance available to us all once we experience our own lighted beingness.

To find the light, go into the darkness. To live the light, move through the pain. To be in truth, consume illusion. May your fire set you free.

RESOURCES

School of Actualism Lightwork Centers

San Diego Center
1521 Eagle Lane
El Cajon CA 92020
(619) 562-0749

Escondido Center
1240 S. Hale #45
Escondido CA 92025
(619) 743-5240

Coast Center
1535 Baker St.
Costa Mesa CA 92626
(714) 957-9346

Los Angeles Center
764 S. Plymouth Blvd.
Los Angeles CA 90005
(213) 935-0849

San Francisco Center
c/o Joan Kanner
2280 Pacific Ave. #502
San Francisco CA 94115
(415) 563-3390

New York Center
27 West 72nd St.
New York NY 10023
(212) 873-5826

Spiritual Emergence Network
250 Grove Ave.
Menlo Park CA 94025
(415) 327-2776

Our work on this planet is about spiritual emergence. If yours is producing psychological disturbances, this is a valuable referral service for individuals in need of assistance in this realm.

Jane Evans Latimer
c/o LivingQuest
Box 3306-B
Boulder CO 80307
(303) 444-1319

For a list of private teachers of inner light-fire in various parts of the country, information on Jane's tape series or workshops, a free catalog of books and tapes on personal transformation and spiritual awakening, or if you would like to sponsor an Inner Light-Fire Workshop, contact the above address.

SUGGESTED READING

At a Journal Workshop by Ira Progoff. Dr. Progoff has developed a unique method of journal writing. The Intensive Journal process is a series of progressive exercises (daily log, twilight imagery, time-stretching, dialoguing and more) which will help you reconnect with the inner content and continuity of your life. An exceptional method.

Bradshaw On: The Family by John Bradshaw. Focuses on the dynamics of the family, how the rules and attitudes learned while growing up become encoded within each family member. Shows how the dysfunctional family system is handed down from one generation to another, creating massive dysfunction within our society. This book guides us out of dysfunction to wholeness and teaches us that false conditioning can be remedied. Families are healed as we as individuals are healed.

Bridge of Light by LaUna Huffines. Offers practical ways of handling the new, intense energies that come with all spiritual expansion. These unique processes were given to the author by a spiritual guide. Included are instructions for meditations, visualizations and psychological techniques to: contact and use the counsel of your higher self; energize your body with light; create your own Temple of Light; receive telepathic messages from higher dimensions; and build Bridges of Light to people or qualities you want to bring into your life.

The Dance of Anger by Harriet Goldhor Lerner, Ph.D. Illuminates the causes and patterns of anger while providing specific strategies for making meaningful and lasting change in our lives. An insightful and prescriptive guide that teaches women how to turn anger into a constructive force for reshaping their lives.

Discovering Your Soul's Purpose by Mark Thurston. You were born with a specific mission in life. Your purpose involves a special way of reaching out to serve others and of reaching inward to nurture yourself. Using techniques described in the Edgar Cayce readings and other spiritual systems, this book outlines practical procedures for discovering your soul's purpose.

Do I Have To Give Up Me To Be Loved By You? by Jordan Paul, Ph.D. and Margaret Paul, Ph.D. Learn about conflict resolution — how to free yourself from the arguing and blaming ways that hold you rigidly trapped within the walls of your conditioning, blocking you from experiencing greater intimacy and love in your life. This book inspires us with the knowledge that personal freedom plus intimacy between partners is a possible and attainable dream.

Embracing Our Selves by Hal Stone, Ph.D. & Sidra Winkelman, Ph.D. An in-depth study of the many selves that make up our personality system.

Focusing by Eugene T. Gendlin, Ph.D. Describes a new technique of self therapy that teaches you to identify and change the way your personal problems concretely exist in your body. Not merely "getting in touch with your feelings," *Focusing* is an effective guide for moving in awareness throughout the body.

Hands of Light: A Guide to Healing Through the Human Energy Field by Barbara Ann Brennan. An in-depth study of the human energy field and chakra system, it shows how the energy field looks, functions, is healed and interacts with others. It provides training in the ability to see and interpret auras, gives guidelines for healing the self and others, and is rich with the author's personal life adventure.

Healing the Child Within by Charles L. Whitfield, M.D. Outlines some basic principals for discovering the True Self, the Child Within. Specifically written for those who come from dysfunctional families, this book will help anyone who is having trouble accessing their highest potential.

Healing the Shame That Binds You by John Bradshaw. Through the use of affirmations, visualizations, "inner voice," "feeling" work and guided meditations, we are shown how to heal the shame that binds us to our compulsions, codependencies and addictions.

Inner Work by Robert A. Johnson. In-depth instruction on how to work with dreams and "active imagination." Good for anyone who wants more understanding of the array of our inner selves.

Joy's Way by W. Brugh Joy, M.D. Dr. Joy's life-threatening disease led him to a profound illumination which caused him to give up his medical practice abruptly. Six weeks later he discovered his illness was miraculously cured. This pushed him to explore further into new realms of healing involving body energies, the energy field, the chakra system, meditation and higher levels of consciousness. His book shows the process of individual and group transformation and contains fascinating and beautiful insights into the awakening process, meditation and healing, transformational psychology and the transformation of humanity.

Living Binge-Free by Jane Evans Latimer. Written by the author of *The Healing Power of Inner Light-Fire*, this is her personal testimony that complete recovery from eating disorders is possible. Practical steps and exercises embody her process to freedom and are highly useful for those in recovery from any food related issue.

Opening to Inner Light by Ralph Metzner, Ph.D. Looks at the metaphors, symbols and analogies essential to describing the transformation process. A dozen or so occur over and over in major cultures and sacred traditions throughout the world. This book is a scholarly work that draws upon the writings of Eastern and Western mysticism, comparative mythology, literature and poetry, and philosophers and teachers in the esoteric, shamanic, yogic and hermetic traditions. It incorporates the formulations of modern depth psychotherapy, anthropology and transpersonal psychology.

Paradox of Power: Balancing Personal and Higher Will by Mark Thurston. The secret of power is found in the human will — that elusive, misunderstood ingredient of the human soul.

The Healing Power of Inner Light-Fire

This book describes the will as (1) that aspect of the self that gives us the power to create our way in life; and (2) the receptive aspect that puts us in touch with a higher, spiritual power. Using many practical examples from daily living, this book shows the seven qualities of a healthy will and describes the five stages of will development. Learn ways to receive guidance from a higher will and for finding your soul's mission on earth.

Transformers: The Therapists of the Future by Jacquelyn Small. A book for and about the process of guiding others in the transformational journey. It describes the therapeutic attitude for the coming age and gives guidelines for the awakening process that expands our unrealized potential as conscious human beings.

What We May Be by Piero Ferrucci. The first comprehensive guide to psychosynthesis as developed by Dr. Robert Assaglio. Outlines techniques for psychological and spiritual growth. Work with subpersonalities, will and intuition is emphasized. Special in its emphasis on the higher aspects of man.

All of the books listed in this section are available from LivingQuest. Please write for a free catalog and information on Jane Evans Latimer's audiocassette series on healing with inner light-fire. Box 3306-B, Boulder CO 80307, or call (303) 444-1319 to order by Visa, MasterCard or Discover.

INDEX